MY BANNED BLACK HISTORY SERMONS

Sermons about Jesus that Christian Nationalists Reject

By Rev. Amiri B. Hooker

South Carolina United Methodist Advocate Press

Advocate Press

First published in the United States of America in 2024
by the South Carolina United Methodist Advocate Press.

Library of Congress Cataloging-in-Publication Data
My Banned Black History Sermons
p. cm.

Cover photo: Paul Palmer

ISBN 979-8-9883575-4-4

Dedication

This is dedicated to the powerhouse women who infuse my world with womanist energy. To Claudette, my megastar mother, always dropping comments on my sermons on Facebook. Valerie, my fierce wife, your grace fuels my revolution. To my unstoppable daughters, powerful aunts, and the celestial angels who bring their magic.

Table of Contents

Foreword vii

Preface... xi

Introduction xv

Chapter 1: Location Is as Important as Breathing 1

Chapter 2: It's Not What They Call You but What You Answer To..................... 11

Chapter 3: Hollywood and Films Have Not Gotten It Right........................ 21

Chapter 4: Higher Education and the Miseducation of the Church Negro.......... 29

Chapter 5: Who Has the Rock Next? 36

Chapter 6: The Real Question is What Color You Will Decide to Represent....... 42

Chapter 7: The Key to Peace is Color Blindness 49

Chapter 8: The Powerful Need to Remember to Forgive................................ 57

Chapter 9: We Need to Move Forward Together, Not One Step Back 65

Chapter 10: Let's Talk About Real Liberation and Liberation Theology.............73

Conclusion... 81

Appendix: Roll Call of Preachers Who Might Be Banned............................. 83

Bibliography.. 91

About the Author.. 97

Foreword

Banning is as old as human civilization, as old as sin. Whenever and wherever people take advantage of others—using people for egocentric and ethnocentric gain—the exclusion that is banning shows up.

Note that as old as it is, it is not natural. Subjugation is certainly old but, as old as it is, rebellion against it is the same age. The loss of freedom requires acquiescence at some minimal level. Such acquiescence does not last long. God placed opposition to repression in every human soul. All humans crave God's self-evident gift of freedom. Opposition to repression always shows up.

Thus, for those bent on oppressing people, banning is the name of the game. Barring ideas, preventing opinions, thwarting of any and all notions that emancipate people is a necessity. Dictators maintain their tyrannies by controlling conversation, communication, freedom, and even life. This politics of belief prohibition—biblical, partisan, historical, and contemporary —shows itself repeatedly in the annals of history.

An extremely short list of governmentally isolated people (those banned, arrested, sanctioned) because of sharing thoughts believed to be incendiary includes such icons and legends as Jesus of Nazareth; John the Revelator; Martin Luther, progenitor of Protestantism; Michael Servetus, challenger of Trinitarian doctrine; David Walker, with his *Appeal, in Four Articles; Together with a Preamble, to the Colored Citizens of the World, but in Particular, and Very Expressly, to Those of the United States of America*; Nelson Rolihlahla Mandela, former president of South Africa; Robert Sobukwe, cofounder of the Pan Africanist Congress; Winnie Madikizela-Mandela, mother of South African freedom; Steve Biko, the Black consciousness prophet; Donald Woods, South African journalist; Fannie Lou Hamer, Mississippi freedom fighter; Rosa Parks, mother of the civil rights movement; Dr. Martin Luther King Jr.; Fred Hampton, Black Panther Party leader; and Angela Davis, scholar activist.

Note that several of these banned were also killed. The politics of assassination is the ultimate banning.

Oppressors target ideas when they cannot quite get away with arrests or execution. Books, pamphlets, essays, and even songs have been banned regularly. "Strange Fruit," recorded by Billie Holiday; *The Color Purple* by Alice Walker; *The Great Gatsby* by F. Scott Fitzgerald; *Beloved* by Toni Morrison; *Native Son* by Richard Wright; *The Diary of a Young Girl* by Anne Frank; *Go Tell It on the Mountain* by James Baldwin; *Their Eyes Were Watching God* by Zora Neale Hurston; *Invisible Man* by Ralph Ellison; *The Grapes of Wrath* by John Steinbeck; *To Kill a Mockingbird* by Harper Lee—these are among works banned in the United States because they were feared by "the powers that be."

These lyrics and texts discomforted autocrats. Their despotic administrations could not stand the challenges offered to the way things were. Beyond those mentioned, other banning evidence exists in U.S. history. In 1650, prominent Massachusetts Bay colonist William Pynchon's *The Meritorious Price of Our Redemption* was deemed heretical. The government burned his pamphlet and banned it. In the 1850s, when multiple states outlawed anyone expressing anti-slavery sentiments, Harriet Beecher Stowe's *Uncle Tom's Cabin* was also banned and burned. Such censorship extends now into the 21st century.

In 2023, a South Carolina educator feared returning to school to teach after being reported to the school board for teaching an all-White Advance Placement class about racism, using Ta-Nehisi Coates's *Between the World and Me*.[1] Forbidding certain viewpoints is a deep rooted and present-day reality. This reality serves authorities, those devoted to maintaining the existing state of affairs. Outlawing opinions and closeting certain concepts assures control for the powerful controllers.

Sermons then, in the eyes of those who would dominate others, must especially be banned. Situations change; contexts are shaken by preaching and preachers. Contrary to present days, sermons are not meant to be nice, entertaining orations for feeling good alone. Many pulpits operate largely for performance, unifying persons around amusement; however, that is not the meaning of nor the reason for preaching.

Regarding evil and harm, sermons are dangerous.

Preaching, according to Isaac R. Clark Jr., is "a substantially divine activity, wherein the word of God is proclaimed or announced on contemporary issues, with a view towards ultimate response to our God."[2] Preaching is meant to broadcast God's position on current situations and issues. It offers more than diagnosis. Preaching offers solutions, expecting the hearers to respond, to do something because of what they heard.

---

1. Hannah Natanson, "Her Students Reported Her for a Lesson on Race. Can She Trust Them Again?" *The Washington Post.* September 18, 2023. https://www.washingtonpost.com/education/2023/09/18/south-carolina-teacher-ta-nehisi-coates-racism-lesson/.

2. Katie Geneva Cannon, *Teaching Preaching Isaac Rufus Clark and Black Sacred Rhetoric* (Eugene, OR: Cascade Books, 2015), 41.

Such preaching frightens the oppressor and any who love things the way they are. It unsettles those who protect, will live for, and will even die for the status quo. People who hear the word of God—who are motivated, enlightened, invigorated, and encouraged by the power of the good news to liberate minds and souls—cannot and will not relax into an opiated state of the ordinary. Fear of change makes this censorship a necessary tactic for maintaining power relationships.

By uplifting the history and contributions of Black people, this collection of sermons challenges the sin of racism. It exists to empower through information and inspiration. Amiri Hooker connects them to the biblical drama and offers hope to any who read. Only those who want things to stay as they are—Black people relegated to the political, economic, and religious underclass—will have problems with this work.

We can never forget that Jesus suffered ultimate banishment in his crucifixion. He was arrested, tortured, and executed because his ideas tore at the fabric of oppression. He told a subjugated people to embrace their full humanity and said God made them to be more than footstools of a domineering system. Jesus offered life to a people whose society promised only slow death. He was crucified because his words gave truth, hope, and pride.

This is what Pastor Hooker does in these sermons. Homiletically, he offers the truth, hope, and pride that Christ gave him to share. He speaks historical realities, and their biblical implications, that are essential to the Black community. This truth is crucial to the nation and the world because, without it, the nation loses its soul, and a soulless nation cannot benefit the planet.

I invite you, therefore, to read these sermons. Sit with them and let them sit with you. See why they have found their way into the pantheon of banned ideas, and therefore why they must be read, especially by disciples of Jesus Christ.

If you believe in freedom, these sermons will permeate your eternal soul if you let them. They resonate with any who believe in grace and faith, who stand for self-respect and nobility, who live out the gospel demands of love and justice.

If seeking sermonic discourse that merely humors and placates, this text is not for you; however, if you want to read preachments that declare God's preference for the marginalized many, you will love reading this book.

—The Reverend Dr. Vance P. Ross, senior pastor of Central United
Methodist Church, Atlanta; former director of annual conference
relationships for Discipleship Ministries; first deputy general secretary for
Discipleship Ministries; and former senior pastor of Gordon Memorial UMC,
Nashville, Tennessee, and First UMC, Hyattsville, Maryland

Preface

I normally spend weeks working on sermons during February because it is Black History Month; I feel there is a need to increase the content and connection the congregation gets from the culturally informative sermons and illustration. At the same time, I am appreciative of the Black history moments that are encouraged in each church.

Black history moments normally only recant the most famous national African-American history figures. A good pastor is responsible for bringing something extra to their preaching table during February. Nevertheless, the first Sunday in February 2022 was unique because we had a guest speaker coming in, so I had not prepared a sermon for the upcoming worship celebration.

About 10 o'clock that Thursday morning, I received a call that my speaker for that Sunday had gotten snowed in and was not going to make it. Thus, I began working on a sermon. It would have to be good because the folk were expecting something special from a guest speaker.

That is where the concept of a series of sermons, #MyBlackHistory, came from.

#MyBlackHistory was a series of sermons that looked at the Bible as a way of connecting discipleship to the Mother Continent. It was a way showing that Christianity is not a White man's religion and that Africa was the cradle of civilization and the springboard of the American Black Christian church. The #MyBlackHistory sermon series was also a way of demonstrating that the Black church was more than an invisible institution born in the midst of slavery.

But what a surprise I encountered when, on Sunday morning, I learned a sermon I'd posted late Friday night had been rejected from a sermon hosting site—a site I had used for more than twelve years.

Sermon-hosting sites offer clergy members like me an unprecedented opportunity to reach a global audience. Through the internet, individuals from different parts of the world can access sermons and teachings, transcending geographical boundaries.

This level of accessibility enables clergy to touch the lives of people they may never meet in person, spreading their message of hope, faith, and love far beyond the confines of their local congregation.

Sermon hosting sites also serve as virtual archives for the sermons delivered by clergy members. These social media platforms preserve valuable teachings, making them accessible for future reference or study. As a result, clergy can build a repository of their spiritual insights, allowing their wisdom to endure and be shared across generations. The longevity of sermons ensures that the impact of a clergy member's words extends far beyond their immediate delivery time.

I intentionally omitted the mention of the sermon hosting site I employed. This choice is deliberate, as I aim to prevent any negative repercussions for this commendable platform dedicated to sermon sharing. Furthermore, I acknowledge that the hosting site is affiliated with a major multimillion-dollar company. Considering their corporate stature, they may find it more expedient to pursue legal measures against a smaller pastor rather than address public scrutiny of their policies. But it says on its website that it "is the world's leader in sermon resources and research, dedicated to equipping pastors worldwide in excellence in preaching." One of the proudest moments I recall in ministry is when one of my daughters in ministry called and told me she had been having problems finding Black history sermons to study, and found only one on the major sites, but it was mine and she loved it. I have sermons on that site that were viewed more than thirty-two thousand times. I had never had a sermon rejected.

And I never dreamed my sermon would be rejected because of a theological assumption that seemed to suggest both White privilege and a true lack of understanding of the Black church tradition and preaching practice.

In the rejection, I was told, "We have to reject your sermon because of the premise that Jesus and all his disciples were African. This is not what the scriptures teach. He was not African or White Anglo-Saxon. He was a Jew from the tribe of Judah in a small town named Bethlehem. He grew up in Nazareth and spent a few years living in Egypt as a child. His entire ministry was localized to the Jewish nation of Israel. These are facts beyond dispute as this is what a straightforward reading of the Gospels teaches us. Teaching that Jesus was White or Black falsely represents him. Yes, he is the Savior of the world, of every tribe, tongue, and nation. But he is not Black."

I went on to preach that banned sermon, titled "#MyBlackHistory Does Not Begin with Slavery, It Starts In Africa," to my church that Sunday. It was well received.

But over the next few days, that sermon site reviewed and ultimately rejected any of the fifty-five sermons I had posted on that sermon hosting site mentioning the African origins of biblical characters and any declaration of Jesus as Black.

I understand and respect the rights of any sermon site to publish what is in line with their audience or theological perspective. But as someone with thirty years of preaching experience, twenty of those years ordained in The United Methodist Church, I believe the concept of a Black Jesus is not out of line with scripture.

In the midst of the current climate marked by the surge in White Christian nationalism and evangelical divisiveness, I sense that it's an ideal time to explore the concepts surrounding a cultural perspective of Jesus as Black. This is also a prime time for all faith groups to be exposed to Black history sermons that speak to relevant theologies of the post COVID-19 world.

That is the purpose of this book.

It is my hope that this collection of sermons serves as a gathering of #MyBlackHistory sermons that can contribute to thought-provoking preaching and teaching. My deep desire is for the church to celebrate Black history not only one month a year but all 365 days.

Anyone who preachers or provides leadership in African-American congregations or communities, from ordained elders to laity supply, will find these sermons to be necessary tools for sharing the word of God in historical context with a spirit of empowerment and discipleship.

Introduction

Black sermons carry the essence of African-American history and traditions. The sermons are the pumping blood of the fight for civil rights, the fight against oppression, and the celebration of resilience.

Sermons that unapologetically speak to Black liberation, Black theology, and Black history can provide a more comprehensive spiritual experience, fostering a sense of cultural enrichment and understanding.

Black sermons often draw from unique spiritual and theological perspectives, incorporating elements such as call and response, passionate delivery, and a strong connection to biblical stories of liberation. These perspectives offer a fresh and profound approach to interpreting religious texts, which can enrich the spiritual lives of people from all backgrounds.

Black history is seamlessly woven into the fabric of almost every sermon in the Black church. In the Black church tradition, from powerful sermons to uplifting gospel music, African Americans' historical contributions to spirituality and music are celebrated year-round. Black history is not confined to a single month or a series of lectures. It is an integral part of the faith, deeply rooted in the fabric of worship, preaching, and community life. A year-round celebration of Black history fosters sermons that are essential to making Black lives—and Black church—matter.

In today's interconnected world, where technology plays a pivotal role in connecting people across different cultures and backgrounds, it is essential to recognize and celebrate diversity in all its forms. One aspect of diversity that has been gaining increasing recognition and appreciation is topical sermons on social issues, which offer richness and depth. These spiritual social justice messages, rooted in African-American history and culture, offer unique perspectives and insights that have the power to enrich the discipleship landscape for all. Black history sermons can provide a glimpse of diversity not seen in other types of sermons.

The practice of banning any form of writing is a form of censorship, with motives ranging from political to legal, religious, moral, or (less often) commercial. In many territories, distribution, promotion, or certain translations of the Bible have historically been prohibited or impeded. Many countries throughout the world have their own methods of restricting access to books, although the prohibitions vary strikingly from one country to another. Yet there seems to be little scholarship devoted to banning sermons.

Despite the opposition from the American Library Association, books continue to be banned by schools and public libraries across the United States. This is usually the result of complaints from parents who find particular books inappropriate for their children (e.g., books about human sexuality or sexual identity, such as *And Tango Makes Three*). Many books that face challenges have themes about race or are by Black authors.

Sermons and religious teaching have not always faced the same type of ridicule and demonization. However, America and its church have changed in recent years, and the need for this book is indeed proof of that change. Sermon-banning advocates argue that it is necessary. They believe religious institutions should not have the power to influence political matters and that sermons, at times, may cross the line into political advocacy.

Biblical Black history sermons often emphasize empowerment and the belief in the capacity to overcome challenges. These sermons can inspire their users to face life's difficulties with courage and determination.

Many Christian nationalists and evangelical White supremacist groups raise arguments over the potential manipulation of congregants for political gain, undermining democratic processes and promoting a particular agenda under the guise of religious teachings. Furthermore, these supremacist groups argue that banning sermons would protect vulnerable individuals from potential hate speech or discriminatory messages that might be propagated in some places of worship. They assert that limiting the influence of Black and liberal religious leaders over their followers would promote greater tolerance and social cohesion.

I vehemently disagree. Sermons are a vital aspect of religious expression and should be protected as a form of free speech—and not only on a governmental level. By banning sermons, institutions are overstepping their boundaries and interfering in spiritual matters, potentially setting a dangerous precedent. Social media platforms have become a central space for people to express their beliefs, share ideas, and engage in discussions on various topics, including religion. Conversely, the spread of misinformation, hate speech, and extremist content has prompted a heated debate on whether religious thought should be banned or restricted on these platforms. Yet even on social media platforms, banning religious thought like sermons altogether raises concerns about violating the principle of free speech, which is a fundamental democratic value.

It is crucial to distinguish between respectful religious discourse and harmful content that incites violence, promotes discrimination, or spreads false information.

The church has never taken a firm position on what to do about misinformation and hate speech. Groups that go against the Bible and discipleship traditions have often been seen as a hidden secret and are often relegated to fringe sects. Like any institution, the church seeks to balance the promotion of freedom of expression with the responsibility to maintain a respectful and loving community.

Historically, the church has tried to steer clear of direct political involvement to preserve its spiritual mission and avoid alienating congregants with diverse political beliefs. Addressing misinformation and hate speech may inadvertently involve the church in political controversies. As extremist religious groups and individuals in the current atmosphere can exploit media platforms to spread their radical ideologies, inciting violence and promoting discrimination, some limits must be set on what can be said. Social media platforms bear the responsibility of moderating content and enforcing community guidelines. Sermon hosting sites bear the same responsibility. Implementing policies that target harmful content, regardless of origin, is vital.

But banning Black history sermons or religious thought in its entirety is not a solution; rather, content moderation teams should focus on identifying and addressing harmful content without infringing on the freedom of expression and freedom of religious doctrine. At some point, we are also going to face the fact that some religious ideas and traditions are incorrect and need to be rooted out of the public debate and social platforms. Yet it must also be clear that no one's speech or religious message should be discounted simply because it presents an alternative or more (or less) biblically correct point of view.

Recently, critical race theory has become a topic of passionate debate and controversy in various fields of society. It is clear the fight around CRT has caused many to question biblical authority and academic theological exploration. While CRT has gained traction in academic circles, its relevance and implications within the Black church have also been a subject of discussion. As an influential institution in the African-American community, the Black church must consider the potential impact of CRT on its mission, theology, and activism. While the intentions behind discussing CRT in churches might be to address racial disparities and promote social justice, some have raised concerns about how this theory influences the celebration of Black history.

CRT, an academic concept taught mostly to law students, has been catapulted into the public dialogue and become the catch-all phrase of those seeking to censor educational discussions dealing with race or racial justice in American schools. From the rapid passage of deeply concerning legislation barring the accurate teaching of America's history in classrooms around the country, to sweeping book bans and threat-laden attacks at school board meetings and against school administrators, the fearmongering around what politically motivated forces are claiming is CRT has starkly illustrated the ever-shifting weapons being leveled at our multiracial democracy.

CRT offers a framework to comprehend the enduring impact of slavery, segregation, and systemic racism on the Black community. By acknowledging our historical trauma, the Black church can better understand the root causes of existing disparities and foster healing and reconciliation. Embracing critical race theory enables the Black church to strengthen its social justice initiatives. By leveraging a deeper understanding of systemic racism, the church can lead and support advocacy efforts aimed at dismantling unjust systems and promoting equity for all.

Recently, a number of conservative Christian leaders agreed the church should be against the spread of CRT. In fall 2020, the presidents of the five Southern Baptist seminaries issued a statement saying that "affirmation of Critical Race Theory, Intersectionality and any version of Critical Theory" is incompatible with the Baptist Faith and Message, the denomination's core beliefs.[1] In recent years, some have identified CRT as an ascendant ideology in the church that is fundamentally at odds with the Christian faith. This anxiety has been mirrored by many conservatives at large, and the debate over this ideology has moved from public disgust to state legislative measures that would ban it in schools.

In context, the rise of racial conflict around CRT comes after the deaths of George Floyd and Breonna Taylor. The social climate around police brutality and misuse of violence spurred both conversations about how the church ought to respond to racial injustice and how the church should discuss the need for CRT policies. Sermon banning is just one more way Christian nationalists and alt-right evangelicals are attempting to downplay the existence of White supremacy in the current church environment.

Pastor Tony Evans, who is African-American, released a statement clarifying his views on CRT after Southern Baptist Convention leaders denounced the theoretical framework for conflicting with the denomination's faith confession—appearing to contradict their denomination's prior resolution on the matter.

As Evans said, "I again affirm that the Bible must be the basis for analyzing any and all social, racial, or political theories to identify what is legitimate or not. But I did not say, nor imply, that CRT or other ideologies lack beneficial aspects—rather, the Bible is the basis for determining that. I have long taught that racism, and its

---

1. George Schroeder, "Seminary Presidents Reaffirm BFM, Declare CRT Incompatible," *Baptist Press,* November 30, 2020. https://www.baptistpress.com/resource-library/news/seminary-presidents-reaffirm-bfm-declare-crt-incompatible/.

ongoing repercussions, are real and should be addressed intentionally, appropriately, and based on the authority of God's inerrant word."[2]

Any disagreement over approaches to racism, such as interpretations of Black Lives Matter or discussions of White privilege, has been conflated with CRT in the minds of many.

We must make certain that our zeal to clarify what we think about CRT is accompanied by a pledge to fight against all forms of discrimination, to make clear that we stand with our brothers and sisters of color in their suffering, lamenting the pain of their past, and to work tirelessly for justice in our present. According to a 2020 Lifeway Research study, 74 percent of pastors agree that their congregation would welcome a sermon on racial reconciliation, with 32 percent strongly agreeing.[3] This is down from 2016, when 90 percent of pastors believed their congregation would be open to a sermon on the topic, with 57 percent strongly agreeing.

Further, 17 percent of pastors say their church would not want to hear about racial reconciliation, up from 7 percent in 2016.

The more the church defends sexism, racism, and White supremacy, the more it seems clear that there is a real fear of change, truth, and historic correction in the current church. Pastors who have already preached on issues of race, including pastors who have received negative feedback for those sermons, believe their congregation would welcome more on the topic. Meanwhile, those who have stayed away from the topic are more divided. Even among pastors who actually did receive negative feedback, 76 percent say their church would be open to sermons on racial reconciliation again.

The pulpit in the Black church is free to discuss social issues, generally. The Black church sees pastors as called by God and therefore free to preach on any topics addressed in the Bible unhindered. Rarely is there pushback about any biblical topic. However, in this day of social media sermons and YouTube worship services, Black pastors have experienced criticism and engaging feedback. Generally, the people in Black churches respond to sermons on racial reconciliation well, but there is occasionally pushback with some comments behind their backs and others wanting to have lunch to lay out their viewpoint.

Some of the most recent pushback seems scripted directly from the anti-CRT evangelicals we see popping up in school board meetings nationally. Sermons and teaching about CRT invite the Black church to reevaluate its theology in the context of racial justice. It challenges the church to consider how doctrines, teachings, and

---

2. Tony Evans, "Race and Reconciliation (Sermon Only)," *YouTube*, December 2, 2020, https://www.youtube.com/watch?v=kW9LxQ33nZE.

3. Aaron Earls, "Pastors More Reluctant to Preach on Race," *Christianity Today*, January 12, 2021, https://www.christianitytoday.com/news/2021/january/pastors-reluctant-preach-racial-reconciliation-lifeway-surv.html.

interpretations may have been influenced by oppressive ideologies and encourage a more inclusive and liberating theology.

About the organization of this book

This book is divided into chapters. Each chapter starts with the sermon title and the sermon site tag that includes the number of views, the date of submission, and the denomination.

Following the site tag, each chapter features an updated introduction that explains the nature of the sermon and why the sermon is still relevant and significant for discipleship in the church.

The next major feature of the chapter is an excerpt of the rejection, as well as the reflection section, which looks at the criteria for banning the sermon and a scholarly reflection on the need to understand why the rejected information needed to be included in the text.

Each chapter ends with the full sermon as initially published on the sermon site.

Please understand that these sermons were created to be preached in a local church and not as a formal manuscript. Many times footnotes and highlights had to be removed while uploading the sermons to the hosting site.

The book concludes with a message of hope for preaching sermons that go beyond the normal and challenge disciples to "float like a butterfly, sting like a bee."

Chapter 1
Location Is as Important as Breathing

"If you do not know where you come from, then you don't know where you are, and if you don't know where you are, then you don't know where you're going. And if you don't know where you're going, you're probably going wrong."
—Terry Pratchett, I Shall Wear Midnight[1]

"I have great respect for the past. If you don't know where you've come from, you don't know where you're going. I have respect for the past, but I'm a person of the moment. I'm here, and I do my best to be completely centered at the place I'm at, then I go forward to the next place."—Maya Angelou[2]

Sermon Site Media Tag: #MyBlackHistory Does Not Begin
with Slavery, It Starts In Africa
Contributed by Amiri Hooker, Feb. 4, 2022
536 views before rejection(Please note this was in two days)
Scripture: Luke 5:1-3
Denomination: United Methodist

About the sermon:

The sermon "#MyBlackHistory Does Not Begin with Slavery, It Starts in Africa" was one of four Black history sermons written during Black History Month 2022. The purpose of the sermon was to highlight the history of Africa and the connection with the Black church. The history of Africa is deeply intertwined with the

---

1. Terry Pratchett, *I Shall Wear Midnight*, (New York: Random House, 2011).
2. Randy Cordova, "Maya Angelou's 2011 'Arizona Republic' Interview," *The Arizona Republic*, May 28, 2014, https://www.azcentral.com/story/entertainment/books/2014/05/28/maya-angelou-arizona-republic-inter-view/9682587/.

story of the Black church, a significant institution that emerged from the struggle for freedom and identity during the African diaspora. From its roots in Africa to its development in the Americas and beyond, the Black church has played a major role in celebrating cultural heritage, advocating for civil rights, and fostering a sense of community.

This sermon was written to make real the global nature of the discipleship of Jesus in the modern world we live. The global community is shaped by interconnectedness and interdependence among people from various regions and cultures. The relationship between Africans on the continent and Africans in the diaspora is a crucial aspect of this interconnectedness. Acknowledging and taking this connection seriously is vital for fostering unity, solidarity, and shared progress.

In this sermon and the series, there is an underlining hope to connect Blacks in America with Blacks on the content of Africa and throughout the diaspora.

Rejection:

"We have to reject your sermon because of the premise that Jesus and all his disciples were African. This is not what the scriptures teach. He was not African or White Anglo-Saxon. He was a Jew from the tribe of Judah in a small town named Bethlehem. He grew up in Nazareth and spent a few years living in Egypt as a child. His entire ministry was localized to the Jewish nation of Israel. These are facts beyond dispute, as this is what a clear reading of the Gospels teaches us. Teaching that Jesus was White or Black falsely represents him. Yes, he is the Savior of the world, of every tribe, tongue, and nation. But he is not Black."

Reflections:

The three most important considerations in real estate: Location. Location. Location. This is not just true in real estate. It's also true in life, faith, and scripture interpretation. The location has much to do with how we read and understand the Bible.

Humans first evolved in Africa, and much of human evolution occurred on that continent. The fossils of early humans who lived between six million and two million years ago come entirely from Africa. The Out of Asia theory is a scientific theory that contends that modern humans first arose in Asia. Until the mid-20th century, most anthropologists preferred Asia over Africa as the continent where the first hominids evolved. The recent African origin of modern humans ("Out of Africa") theory is better supported by available data. In Cheikh Anta Diop's book *The African Origin of Civilization: Myth or Reality*, he asks whether Egyptian civilization could be of Asian origin:

Here, as in all that has preceded, it is important to distinguish between what can be deduced from a strict examination of historical documents and what is claimed over and beyond those documents—contrary to their testimony. To assign Egyptian civilization an Asiatic or any foreign origin whatsoever, we must be able to demonstrate the prior existence of a cradle of civilization outside of Egypt. However, we cannot overemphasize the fact that this basic, indispensable condition has never been met.[3]

The Black church has a long history of challenging systemic injustices faced by African Americans. Black power theology continues this tradition by acknowledging the deeply entrenched racial disparities that persist in various spheres of life. Through sermons and activism, the theology encourages the Black community to unite and confront these inequalities head-on, advocating for social, economic, and political change. The narrative of Black church history is not confined solely to the shackles of slavery but rather traces its profound roots to a time before the transatlantic journey began.

To understand the vibrant tapestry of the Black church, we must delve into the centuries-old history that predates the dark days of bondage. Long before the tragedy of the Middle Passage, the history of the Black church was taking shape in the lands of Africa. The continent was home to a diverse array of cultures and civilizations, each nurturing its unique religious practices and spiritual beliefs. From ancient Egypt to the kingdoms of Ghana, Mali, and Songhai, the people of Africa held profound spiritual connections with the divine. These early African societies saw the rise of intricate religious systems, community gatherings, and sacred spaces where worship, healing, and guidance occurred. The interplay of music, dance, and storytelling laid the foundations for the vibrant expressions of faith that would later flourish in the New World. The brutal transatlantic slave trade brought millions of Africans to the Americas, where they faced unimaginable hardships and cruelty.

Amid this suffering, the resilience of African spirituality and faith endured. Despite the oppressive conditions, the enslaved African community clung to their cultural traditions and religious practices, covertly finding solace in their shared beliefs.

The Black church emerged as an underground network of hope, a sacred space where the enslaved could find spiritual freedom amid their physical chains. In the hush of night, in the secrecy of gatherings, they found strength in their faith, believing in a God who transcended the limitations of their earthly existence. This church, however, was not a new creation but a continuation of the faith and practices that had been generated on the Mother Continent of Africa.

The 1619 Project, launched in 2019 by *The New York Times Magazine*, has been a groundbreaking initiative that seeks to redefine the narrative of American history by placing the year 1619 and the arrival of the first enslaved Africans in the British

3. Cheikh Anta Diop, *The African Origin of Civilization*, ed. Mercer Cook (Chicago: Chicago Review Press, 1989), 100. Kindle.

North American colonies at the center of its exploration. As the 1619 Project seeks to create a more inclusive and accurate portrayal of history, it inherently aligns with the interests of Black church studies. The Black church has been intertwined with the history of African Americans, and its experiences parallel those explored in the 1619 Project. By engaging with the project's findings, scholars in the Black church can further enrich their understanding of the struggles and triumphs of their community.

I asked many of my clergy friends and laity leadership to read the 1619 Project to gain insight into their role of discipleship in the church. The 1619 Project was included in this sermon to bring forth the untold stories of resilience and resistance among enslaved Africans and their descendants. However, it also can help members delve into overlooked narratives of faith, worship, and activism within the Black church.

In attempting to preach a version of this sermon, one needs to be well versed in the information found in *The 1619 Project: A New Origin Story*.[4] It was only after reading the book, and books in opposition to the book, that I was able to lead discussion with my members and trusted friends to develop the ideas for many of the main points in this sermon.

Another preparation for this sermon came from looking at some of the arguments around critical race theory. Embracing CRT enables the Black church to strengthen its social justice initiatives. By leveraging a deeper understanding of systemic racism, the church can lead and support advocacy efforts to dismantle unjust systems and promote equity for all. A true picture of history will only allow the church to do discipleship that makes disciples of all the world.

Reflection follow up:

When this sermon was rejected, I responded with a kind note thinking maybe there was some mistake. I wrote the following:

> I see that my sermon was removed. I was under the understanding that those of us that have contributed for years did not have to have our sermons approved. Secondly, I think the statements by the reader were limited in their declaration of the understanding of Jesus, and I would like to know what scholarship these apparent facts were based on. I am open to differences of opinion but saddened by folks who believe faith is based on seeing things their way and have never been so surprised by the actions of a site I have been on for years.

4. Nikole Hannah-Jones, and The New York Times Magazine, *The 1619 Project: A New Origin Story*, eds. Caitlin Roper, Ilena Silverman, and Jake Silverstein (New York: One World, 2021).

Furthermore, I will share with you some information to show I did not just generate this sermon without doing my study of the points I made.

Scholars like Cain Hope Felder, Cheikh Anta Diop, Walter McCray, and others have spent enormous time and intellectual energies, some making it their life's work, proving that the people of the Bible were not White. On the other hand, very seldom do White scholars feel it necessary to exert any academic endeavor in investigating ancient peoples of European descent to determine the color of their skins; simply by virtue of their European ancestry, they are unquestionably assumed to be White. The aforementioned scholars have more than adequately challenged and refuted the notion that White people comprised the biblical community.

Therefore, this work does not belabor their well-made conclusions, but advances the notion that the people of the Bible were mainly northern Africans and, therefore, Black people. I found this project to be very simple yet extremely complicated. It is simple in that the biblical story begins in Africa, making the biblical Hebrews immediate descendants of Africans. Also, the number of times that Ethiopia, Egypt, and Israel are mentioned in the Bible suggests that the African landmass is referenced more than any other geographical region in biblical times, making it the focus of the biblical story.

Because the histories of Egypt, Ethiopia, and Israel are crucial to the advancements of world civilization, some scholars, despite their impressive academic achievements, are nevertheless locked into the notion of Black inferiority and cannot fathom the reality that these lands are on the continent of Black Africa.

Israel and Egypt are considered Middle East countries. The term "Middle East" entered the English lexicon in the late 19th to early 20th century to designate the area between Arabia and India. Later it was expanded to include, among some Asian nations, the African countries of Egypt, Israel, Morocco, Libya, Algeria, Sudan, Mauritania, and Tunisia, in part to disassociate them from Africa.[5]

I received a follow-up response, which stated in part the following:

Good afternoon, Amiri,

Thank you so much for your thorough response to the issues being discussed. Though I read through all your reply, I want to reply to a few notes that you made. I want to be clear of what I am and am not saying.

---

5. Theron D. Williams, *The Bible is Black History* (Indianapolis, IN: The Bible is Black History Institute, 2020), 13-14, Kindle.

"Some making it their life's work, proving that the people of the Bible were not White."

"Therefore, this work does not belabor their well-made conclusions, but advances the notion that the people of the Bible were mainly northern Africans and therefore, Black people."

"One group claim's that Christianity is not fundamentally a white religion. This is simply historically false."

No serious scholars … claim major characters of Scripture are White. Sure, Europeans would be introduced during the missionary journeys of Paul, but even those people would not be considered "White." Not that White is even a nationality. Regardless, the people from Moses's time to Christ's would be from what we would call the Middle East, even if that is something of a relatively new term. We know what we mean when we use that term.

I don't think that anyone would say that people from Egypt are Black. While the nation might belong to the continent of Africa, they would identify themselves as Egyptian, which has its own unique culture.

I found it unnecessary to respond any further. I realized this was not going to be a theological discourse or debate with a colleague seeking to build the body of Christ to share with the masses for, on many levels, I hold to the idea found in Proverbs 26:4 about argument.

The Banned Sermon:
#MyBlackHistory Does Not Begin with Slavery, It Starts in Africa
By Amiri Hooker, February 4, 2022
Scripture: Luke 5:1-3
Denomination: United Methodist

Sermon text:
Luke 5:1-3 (MSG), "Once when he was standing on the shore of Lake Gennesaret, the crowd was pushing in on him to better hear the Word of God. He noticed two boats tied up. The fishermen had just left them and were out scrubbing their nets. He climbed into the boat that was Simon's and asked him to put out a little from the shore. Sitting there, using the boat for a pulpit, he taught the crowd."

Introduction:
This week, the text invites us to go back to where we started. We can reclaim our

initial acceptance of the faith when we first said yes to Jesus or first said it in public in the presence of a loving and supportive church family. Do you remember when you first heard this amazing, good news, heard it in a way that changed your life? Do you remember when you realized the word of God was meant for you? Hold on to that moment.

Main body:

Why is Jesus important to you? As a fourth-generation schoolteacher, what makes Jesus so powerful to me is that he was a teacher.

That is evident in this text, and I would like to elevate that fact as I ask the larger question: Where does Black history start? This week, I was on social media, and Bakari Sellers posted a message that said Black history started before slavery.

What does that mean? It means that:
• if Jesus taught his disciples; and
• if what he taught them was about their history and heritage; and
• if Jesus taught about Abraham, Isaac, and Jacob; and
• if Jesus taught them about Moses and Miriam and Cain and Abel, or even Adam and Eve;
• then Jesus taught Black history, an African history that was older and more powerful than American chattel slavery.

The question, "Who is Christ?" is one of the most important and challenging questions that must be answered.

The answer must be given by people according to their knowledge of Jesus Christ.

The answer is not a clear-cut answer because everyone gives his or her answer according to his or her experience of Jesus Christ.

Point 1: Jesus Christ has many names. Who is Jesus?

At the time of Jesus's life on earth, there was also a struggle with the question of who Jesus was. He himself even asked this question, "Who do people say I am?" (Matthew 16:13-20; Luke 9:18-21; Mark 8:27-30). People gave answers according to their different knowledge and beliefs about him.

They had different needs and expectations about him. That is why they gave answers that catered to their needs and expectations of that time. Some called him John the Baptist, Elijah, Prophet, and Christ. All of these names carried some expectation of specific actions from Jesus Christ by the people. The people had the privilege of knowing about this man through his works and teachings. Their knowledge and context allowed them to give such answers or names, and even though they were not really sure if they were right or wrong, they continued in their process of naming him.

All those names were not alien to their culture and religion. That is why they were able to come to the conclusion that this is who Jesus was because they had long expected this revelation.

The question—of who Jesus Christ is—is still very problematic for Christians today. The context and the belief are very different from each other, but the problem is the same and still needs an answer.

That is why Jesus Christ is known to some Black Christians only as Son of God, Lord, Savior, Holy God, and even Anointed One, as for them there are no other names that one can use except these names that are in their understanding of the Bible.

What we need to realize is this is what we were taught—that this is how you call Jesus Christ and nothing else. All of these names are used when calling Jesus Christ because one cannot use other names than those revealed to European Christians by the word of God.

We also had some expectations from Jesus Christ because of what we were taught about him by the American/European missionaries who brought the Gospel to the African people and Africans in the United States.

We know God as the only Savior and Lord from the old tradition. But I wonder, church, if we had been raised in Africa, how would we refer to Jesus?

Some African Christians understand Jesus Christ differently. They know him as the Great Ancestor, Powerful Leader, Chief, and Healer. These African Christians believe in naming him differently according to the way they know him and were taught about him from the Bible and through education by their parents. It is not difficult to call him Great Ancestor, Powerful Leader, and Healer because their culture and belief help them to accept him in this way. This is how he has revealed himself to them. This is who he is to them.

Many of us have heard preachers say Jesus is a lawyer in the courtroom, a doctor in the sick room, and this is cultural context.

According to some African Christians, Jesus Christ made himself known uniquely to them in their culture. He cannot be known or understood apart from their cultural context. The relevance of Christ is first appreciated after a time of living in relationship with him.

Point 2: Jesus Is African before the Mayflower

You have to get this. No, I'm not just saying that Jesus has dark skin, which he does, or woolly hair, which he also does. What I am saying is that culturally, when Jesus is studied, he was uniquely African.

This is key because first, it sets up that Africans were Christians before they came to the U.S. as slaves. The 1619 Project invites Black church studies to join its intellectual revolution. In reframing the origins of African-American Christianity, the arrival of African Christians in August 1619 to colonial Virginia and later to colonial Maryland, New York (Dutch New Netherlands), and the Carolinas might become the new inaugural moment of the Black church. Thus, maybe the Black church came before.

The fact that there was African Christianity before "slave religion" of the plantation might serve as a founding source of the Christianity of Black people in North America. Thus, the Black church was not developed in the hush harbors of the coastlands of the plantations, but true African Christianity with an African Jesus crossed the oceans and was central in making American faith real and authentic.

The evidence includes a 1619 letter written by a local Roman Catholic bishop, Manuel Bautista Soares, in which he expressed his outrage that four thousand-plus African Christians from Ndongo in west-central Africa had been captured by "slave traders."[6]

This letter shows, then, a significant presence of African Christians in one of the regions where Africans were captured by slave traders.

The Africans of 1619 came to North America, according to historian John Thornton and other scholars, from one of the most Christianized regions in Africa: the Empire of the Kongo and its neighboring kingdoms of Loango and Ndongo located along or near the west-central African Atlantic coast. By 1619, the Kongolese Empire possessed its own cathedral, churches, lay Christian societies, and schools for girls and boys. Africans also served as Catholic priests, catechists, church musicians, school principals, schoolteachers, court scribes, and Christian monarchs. In the prior century, there even existed a Catholic bishop of Kongolese descent.[7]

If Kongolese Christianity is a major factor in the development of the Black church, then we will need to let the images of the movies *Roots* and *Django*, based on 19th-century slavery, stop serving as the historical backdrop for the Africans of 1619. A new historical context will need to be drawn, and new images will need to be generated.

Point 3: Because of the 1619 Project, do we need new images of Jesus?

• Maybe Black church history can find these new images among the African Christians of the 1620s and 1630s who requested Christian marriage for themselves and baptism for their children.

• Maybe African Christians such as Paulo D'Angola, Elizabeth Key Grinstead,

---

6. David D. Daniels III, "1619 and the Arrival of African Christianity," *Jude 3 Project* (blog), August 31, 2019, https://jude3project.org/blog/slavetrade.

7. E.R. Shipp, "1619: 400 Years Ago, a Ship Arrived in Virginia, Bearing Human Cargo," *USA TODAY*, February 8, 2019.

and others who mounted legal challenges against their enslavement between 1644 and 1656 could be sources of these new images.

• Maybe the small number of African Christians who served as elected officials during the 1600s, such as Mathias de Sousa, a member of the legislature of colonial Maryland from 1641 to 1642, could offer a new set of images.

Along with new images, Black church history could explore the Christian theology and practices that these African Christians introduced to North America during the 1600s. If all African Christians were not first introduced to Christianity by slave masters and their preachers, how do we reconstruct the role that Kongolese Christian theology played in the development of the Black church and American Christianity?

When our mother churches in South Carolina practice healing, prophecy, call-and-response singing, and the ring shout, it's not seen as carryovers from African missiology but true African Christianity.

Point 4: We Need to Preach History of Identity

This is not Simon's first encounter with Jesus in Luke's Gospel. Jesus has already been to Simon's home in Capernaum and has healed his mother-in-law (4:38-39). Perhaps that explains Simon's willingness to let Jesus use his fishing boat as a floating pulpit.

Simon had been fishing all night with no success, then cleaning his nets from the early morning hours. Most likely, he was exhausted and looking forward to going home and getting some sleep. So, it must have seemed a bit of an imposition when Jesus got into Simon's boat and asked him to put out a little way from the shore. Nevertheless, Simon did what Jesus asked (5:1-3).

Luke does not tell us what Jesus taught the crowds that morning. Maybe this is where the church and the tradition have gone wrong. Perhaps instead of focusing on the calling of the disciples and the abundance of the fish, we need to ask the question of what Jesus was teaching.

I want to suggest that in order to get these men to become fishers of other men, Jesus taught them who they were. He taught them of their African heritage and related to them; they learned of him as the Great Ancestor, Powerful Leader, Chief, and Healer. They answered the question of "Who do people say I am?" as they said, "You are the fish provider, the miracle worker, the job creator, the poverty destroyer."

And today, If we are going to take Carter G. Woodson's hope for real, we must tell the story of the real religion of the Africans in America.

We must be like Jesus and remind the Blacks in the church that they are more than an oppressed group that adopted a slavery religion of passivity and pie in the sky.

We have to be like Jesus and call disciples by telling them that they are like their ancestors Abraham, Ebed-Melech, Simon of Cyrene, and Zipporah.

Chapter 2
It's Not What They Call You but What You Answer To

"It ain't what people call you; it's what you answer to."
—Madea's Family Reunion *(2006)[1]*

"The black skin is not a badge of shame,
but rather a glorious symbol of national greatness."
— Marcus Garvey

"I find, in being Black, a thing of beauty:
a joy, a strength, a secret cup of gladness."
— Ossie Davis

Sermon Site Media Tag: Call Me Black
Contributed by Amiri Hooker, March 22, 2011
11 ratings, 38,196 views before rejection
Scripture: Amos 9:6-8
Denomination: United Methodist

About the sermon:

This was one of the first sermons I posted to a social media site, and it took me months to develop. I had been posting sermons to a note section on Facebook and Myspace, but this particular sermon had taken me months to write and was written to be preached at a church in my home community. They had a real influence on my

---

1. Tyler Perry, director, *Madea's Family Reunion*, Lionsgate, 2006.

spiritual growth and development. So, this was a sermon that I felt spoke to some of the major issues I'd struggled with as a child and teenager. The sermon covered issues of self-pride, colorism, racism, and historic correction. It was a sermon that helped define my preaching style.

Excerpt of rejection:
You stated in your sermon that the Bible focuses 80 percent on the continent of Africa. While many events take place in Africa (mainly Egypt), it nevertheless takes place mainly in Asia (the Middle East).

Also, while atheists in the science community may claim that human life started in Africa, we know from the Scriptures that life started in the Garden of Eden located somewhere in Asia (north of Israel to the Black Sea or East of Israel near the Persian Gulf). This is where all humanity descends from (Adam) according to Scripture. Therefore, to say that we are all African is unscriptural.

Reflection:
When someone says something bad about you or to you, they are challenging your self-esteem. How do you see yourself? How valuable do you consider yourself to be? By acknowledging their taunt, by answering to the name they called you, you are lowering your self-esteem, aren't you? By denying their view of you, and standing up for your own view of yourself, you can make your view of yourself the dominant one. If you keep answering to their view of you, you start to make their view of you the dominant one.

Personally, I prefer to control my destiny, as much as any of us do. The person who controls the self-esteem controls the life of the person in question. If you are in control of your self-esteem, you are in control of your life.

The topic of skin color and racism has been a significant issue throughout history, with various societies witnessing discrimination and bias based on skin tones. However, it is essential to consider how the concept of race and its associated prejudices were understood during the time of biblical writing. In the realm of religious identity, language holds immense power in shaping the way communities understand and express their beliefs.

Within The United Methodist Church, the term "Black" has been historically preferred over "African American" by members of the Black community. This preference is rooted in a complex historical context and a desire to reclaim a distinct and empowering identity. The decision to use "Black" instead of "African American" within the UMC traces back to a historical context of racial identity in the United States. During the era of slavery and segregation, African Americans were stripped of their native languages, cultures, and histories, effectively severing their ties to their

African roots. The term "Black" emerged as a way to reclaim a shared identity that transcended geographical origins and emphasized the common experiences of Black Americans.

Growing up in the South, you could almost overlook the subtle indications of blackness as evil or less than. In Latin, a word for black, ater, and to darken, atere, were associated with cruelty, brutality and evil. They were the root of the English words "atrocious" and "atrocity." Black was also the Roman color of death and mourning. For some, black evokes positive associations, including attractiveness and elegance.[2] The color oozes sophistication. That's why so many people choose to don black clothing when attending a fancy event. It's also why high-end brands such as Tiffany & Co. and Chanel utilize black in their logos.[3] When it comes to high society, the color black has long been associated with power, from priests to judges and tuxedos to credit cards. And let's not forget about Steve Jobs.

However, many use the color black to symbolize all things negative. Throughout history, this somber color has been tied to death and all things evil and bad. It evokes strong feelings of anger, aggression, fear, and sadness.

The connection between black and negativity is probably most clearly seen in our language. Just consider these commonly used expressions: black Monday, black plague, black magic, blackball, blackhole, black-hearted, black mood, black sheep, blackmail, black market, blackout. The list could go on.

And nothing says "bad guy" quite like the color black. Though black is worn (and often preferred) by people from all walks of society, it's often seen as the stereotypical color for criminals and villains.

The phrase "black is beautiful" referred to a broad embrace of Black culture and identity. It called for an appreciation of the Black past as a worthy legacy, and it inspired cultural pride in contemporary Black achievements.

In its philosophy, "black is beautiful" focused also on emotional and psychological well-being. The movement affirmed natural hairstyles like the Afro and the variety of skin colors, hair textures, and physical characteristics found in the African-American community.

"Black is beautiful" also manifested itself in the arts and scholarship. Black writers used their creativity to support a Black cultural revolution. Scholars urged Black Americans to regain connections to the African continent. Some studied Swahili, a language spoken in Kenya, Tanzania, and the southeastern regions of Africa.

2. S. Craig Roberts, Roy C. Owen, and Jan Havlicek, "Distinguishing between Perceiver and Wearer Effects in Clothing Color-Associated Attributions," *Evolutionary Psychology*, July 1, 2020, https://doi.org/10.1177/147470491000800304.

3. Martin Amsteus, Sarah Al-Shaaban, Emmy Wallin, and Sarah Sjöqvist, "Colors in Marketing: A Study of Color Associations and Context (in) Dependence," *International Journal of Business and Social Science* 6, no. 3 (March 2015), https://ijbssnet.com/journals/Vol_6_No_3_March_2015/4.pdf.

The Black Aesthetic, edited by scholar Addison Gayle, contains essays that call for Black artists to create and evaluate their works based on criteria relevant to Black life and culture.[4] Their aesthetics, or the values of beauty associated with the works of art, should reflect their African heritage and worldview, not European dogma, the contributors stated. A Black aesthetic would embolden Black people to honor their own beauty and power. This kind of Black aesthetic is a powerful concept that encompasses the artistic and cultural expressions of the African-American community, highlighting its unique experiences, history, and creativity. Emphasizing the importance of teaching the Black aesthetic in the Black church allows for the appreciation and celebration of African-American art, literature, music, and other forms of expression, ultimately fostering a more inclusive and diverse learning environment for all disciples.

During the 1960s and 1970s, the Black Power movement emerged as a response to systemic racism and sought to promote Black pride and empowerment. Leaders such as Malcolm X and the Black Panther Party encouraged embracing the term "Black" as a symbol of resistance against racial prejudice and the reclamation of a positive racial identity. Since then, the term "Black" has been widely adopted by many African Americans as an expression of their heritage and struggle for equality.

Despite efforts to reclaim the term, some people may still find it offensive because of the notion of color blindness. Color blindness suggests that people should not see or acknowledge racial differences, which can be perceived as dismissing the unique experiences and challenges faced by various racial and ethnic groups, including African Americans. Instead of celebrating diversity, color blindness can inadvertently erase cultural identities and perpetuate systemic inequalities. Language is powerful, and the context in which words are used can significantly impact their meaning. While "Black" has become an empowered term for many, using it carelessly or insensitively can cause offense. The intent behind the use of racial terms matters, and it is crucial to be respectful and aware of historical context when discussing race and identity.

In the year 2011, there was no Black Lives Matter movement. #BLM is a powerful civil rights movement that emerged in response to the persistent racial injustices faced by African Americans. At the heart of this movement lies the profound significance of "blackness." For centuries, African Americans have endured discrimination, violence, and marginalization solely based on the color of their skin. Embracing blackness allows the movement to honor the resilience and resistance displayed by generations of Black individuals who fought for freedom, civil rights, and equality.

Most of the Bible does take place on the continent of Africa; 80 percent may have

---

4. "Doctoral Dissertations in Music and Music Education, 1968-1971, *Journal of Research in Music Education,* 20, no. 1 (1972): 2-185, https://www.jstor.org/stable/i276042.

been an understatement. The African continent has long been recognized as one of the cradles of civilization, home to ancient cultures and advanced societies. The Nile River Valley, in particular, was a thriving center of knowledge, trade, and religious expression. From the stories of Moses to the early Christian communities, Africa played a pivotal role in shaping the biblical narrative.

Jerome Gay Jr.'s research highlights the significance of Africa in the story of the Exodus. While the Israelites' journey from Egypt to the Promised Land is well-known, the African context of this narrative is often downplayed. By acknowledging the geographical and cultural ties between ancient Egypt and the broader African continent, Gay emphasizes the importance of understanding the Exodus within its African context.[5] As we delve deeper into the biblical stories set in Africa, we gain a richer understanding of the interconnectedness between faith, history, and the diverse tapestry of humanity.

Eric Mason's work focuses on Christianity's African roots and the contributions of early African Christian communities to the faith's development. From the early days of Christianity, Africa was home to vibrant Christian centers, such as Alexandria and Carthage, which played pivotal roles in theological discussions and scriptural interpretations. Both Gay and Mason delve into the profound connection between Ethiopia and the Bible. The Queen of Sheba's visit to King Solomon, as recorded in the Old Testament, has strong Ethiopian ties. Additionally, the encounter between Philip and the Ethiopian eunuch, which led to his baptism, signifies Africa's crucial role in the spread of early Christianity. Gay and Mason's work challenges Eurocentric interpretations of the Bible that have often overshadowed Africa's significance in the sacred text.

Throughout history, much of Christian theology has been developed and interpreted within Eurocentric contexts. As a result, many evangelical traditions have been influenced by European perspectives, leading to a tendency to overlook or downplay the African origins and settings of biblical stories. This Eurocentrism can perpetuate biases that dismiss the significance of Africa's role in shaping Christianity.

The era of colonialism deeply influenced how Western nations viewed Africa and its history. Colonial powers often portrayed Africa as a place of savagery and un-civilized societies, which further marginalized African contributions to Christianity. These distorted narratives continue to affect some evangelical circles, leading to an unconscious rejection of Africa's connection to the biblical narrative.

While the issues of blackness were not stated in the rejection, the biases are clearly displayed in the nature of the question of biblical geography.

---

5. Jerome Gay, *The Whitewashing of Christianity: A Hidden Past, A Hurtful Present, and A Hopeful Future* (Chicago: 13th and Joan, 2021).

The Banned Sermon:
Call Me Black
By Amiri Hooker, March 22, 2011
Scripture: Amos 9:6-8
Denomination: United Methodist

Scripture text:

Amos 9:5-8 (MSG), "My Master, God-of-the-Angel-Armies, touches the earth, a mere touch, and it trembles. The whole world goes into mourning. Earth swells like the Nile at flood stage; then the water subsides, like the great Nile of Egypt. God builds his palace—towers soaring high in the skies, foundations set on the rock-firm earth. He calls ocean waters and they come, then he ladles them out on the earth. God, your God, does all this. 'Do you Israelites think you're any better than the far-off Cushites?' God's Decree. 'Am I not involved with all nations? Didn't I bring Israel up from Egypt, the Philistines from Caphtor, the Arameans from Qir? But you can be sure that I, God, the Master, have my eye on the Kingdom of Sin. I'm going to wipe it off the face of the earth. Still, I won't totally destroy the family of Jacob.' God's Decree."

Introduction:

This is a sermon for Black History Month 2011, given at Cedar Fall Missionary Baptist Church, Blenheim, South Carolina, with a purpose of dealing with self-pride and the love that God has for all races and people around the world and the need to deal with race and community worldwide.

Main body:

Black is the most misunderstood color. A black-tie dinner is very formal and elegant. Women can wear that "must have little black dress" to the black-tie dinner. Yet the bad guys wear black hats. Black symbolizes death in some cultures. Native Americans thought black was good because it was the color of soil, which gives life.

Yet I have come to notice in recent days that we as a people are falling back into a trap that should have been gone forty or fifty years ago. So for Black history this year, I want to talk about being called Black.

We as a people have been called many things. We have been called Negro, African, Colored, Black, and now African-American. But let's keep it real.

(Do you want some? Then say it with me—give me some!)

The only time we refer to ourselves as African American is when we are writing a paper or putting something in the newspaper. For the most part, we call ourselves

Black. Use of the term "Black" dates to the 1960s and 1970s and the civil rights movement. The Black Power movement advocated strongly for the use of "Black" to replace the outdated "negro," and many Americans of African ancestry started to embrace the term. Others preferred "Afro American," an early blending of "African" and "American." In the 1980s, "African American" began to see common usage, and the term quickly became very popular. But most people I know still use Black.

Point 1: We are all Black

The argument for saying "Black" is that it is a term that refers purely to skin color, recognizing that people from Africa come in various shades and hues. Using "Black" also allows people to distinguish between Americans with slave ancestors, who may not have a close connection with Africa, and recent immigrants from Africa. This term also includes Americans of slave ancestry who immigrated from the Caribbean, as these individuals may feel more closely connected to places such as Haiti or Jamaica than Africa. Thus when we say and use Black, we are referring to all our dark-skinned cousins.

There are some things we just have to accept (OK, say it, give me some). One, the Bible is a story about Africans and their relationship with God. Eighty percent of the Bible deals with the continents of African and African people. It is not until we get to the book of Acts and someone decides to go to Asia Minor that the Bible story leaves the Mother Continent.

Two, I say Mother Continent for a reason as science has proven life started on Africa. The oldest human bones have been found in Africa, the genetic evidence points to Africa (Mitochondrial Eve is African, and Sub-Saharan Africans are the most genetically diverse humans on Earth), and even the first evidence of human culture is found in Africa. Since we were from Africa, it makes sense that the first humans were probably dark skinned, as that protects against skin cancer. Light skin color is a later adjustment to take as much advantage of sunlight as possible in the days before Vitamin D pills. Thus, we all have Black ancestors, and everyone is Black. Just some folks we call White are really just less Black. (Try sharing that next year at your Confederate Day party in South Carolina!) Yes, we must understand we are all Black. Black is our history.

Point 2: Sudan is a lesson for Black people

Some folks have made us feel the term Black is derogatory or a bad thing. I had stopped paying this any attention. For some reason I had forgotten all the jokes and janks and picks we had growing up, picking on folks about being Black, until a few weeks ago I was in my car listening to a briefing on Sudan.

Sudan's ongoing civil war is more than twenty years old. While there have been continuous efforts to stop the war between the Muslim north and Christian south, the Arab government has launched new attacks against Blacks in the country's western Darfur region.

Folks are killing themselves in Sudan. You know, Sudan, this region of Africa just south of Egypt, has significant ties to the Bible. From Moses's wife to the Ethiopian eunuch, people from the Sudan interacted with biblical characters. In the Bible, Sudan is also referred to as Cush, Nubia, and Ethiopia. Often when the Bible mentions a place at the end of the world, it would refer to Sudan (Psalm 87:4). One also has to note all these terms are different ways of saying "the land of the Black." The Cushites, mentioned several times in the Old Testament, prepare the way for this interpretation. The Cushites are clearly Black and African. Professor J. Daniel Hays demonstrates this thoroughly in a recent two-part article.[6] Cush is the land upstream from the fourth cataract of the Nile River in what today is Sudan. This is the area of the great bend in the river as it flows southwest before resuming its northerly flow.

The Greeks called the Black people south of Egypt "Ethiopians," but most of these were Cushites, or Sudanese.

Well, if you haven't noticed that Darfur or Sudan is having a problem, they are killing each other over race. Two million people have been killed during the civil war in the Sudan region of Africa mostly over race, mostly over skin tone. The name Sudan comes from "bilad al sudan," Arabic for "the land of the blacks." All over being called Black.

So, you might expect the Sudanese to be comfortable with the color of their skin. But they're not.

"They are equating Black with dullness, so a Black person is stupid, automatically a slave," says Sudan southerner Agnes Silver Nyarsuk.[7]

She explains that Southern Sudanese consider themselves Black, while northerners see themselves as Arabs—and treat Blacks as second class.

"For transport, an Arab lady when she enters, the men will stand up and give the place, for an Arab lady, because she's a woman," Nyarsuk says. "But a Black lady, even if she is old, and she's shivering, dying, they will not respect because you are automatically a slave."

The differences between north and south might seem like one of religion, but that's only a secondary conflict. Most northerners are Muslims. And most southerners follow traditional African religions or Christianity.

So, I know you want to know how it got that way. Say it now—give me some!

The racism which the British brought, Kitchener planted it here, divided the

6. J. Daniel Hays, "The Cushites: A Black Nation in Ancient History," *Bibliotheca Sacra 153* (July 1996): 270-280.

7. Matthew Brunwasser., "Racism in Sudan," *The World*, PRI, February 7, 2011.

people in the four categories, said the Swedish biologist and physician Carl Linnae-us.[8] It's a tiered system of racism. The top category was the White race, represented by Kitchener and the people he brought. Second was the Arab Egyptians who made up much of his army. Category three were the Sudanese working as porters and servants. And at the bottom were Black southerners.

So it's logical that the post-independence elite who have ruled the country since 1956 see themselves as Arabs. People are killing themselves in the street over being called Black.

But today I say: To the Sudanese, to the Cush, to the African American, to the Blenheimite, there is a word from God. You are Black, and Black is beautiful. As a matter of fact, Black is blessed.

Point 3: There is power in being Black.

Today, the line "Say it loud: I'm Black and I'm proud" may seem like a relatively straightforward message, but together these eight words conveyed a new self-confidence and assertiveness among the Black community in 1968 America. This one powerful line conveys the central message of the song, pushing the music forward. In the song, James Brown tells the children to "say it loud," and with feeling that they are proud of being Black. This is not a message to be whispered but to be proclaimed with confidence, even a bit of swagger.

Another example is the Black Power movement. The Black Power movement instilled a sense of racial pride and self-esteem in Blacks. Blacks were told that it was up to them to improve their lives. Black Power advocates encouraged Blacks to form or join all-Black political parties that could provide a formidable power base and offer a foundation for real socioeconomic progress. For years, the movement's leaders said, Blacks had been trying to aspire to White ideals of what they should be.

Now it was time for Blacks to set their own agenda, putting their needs and aspirations first. An early step, in fact, was the replacement of the word "Negro" (a word associated with the years of slavery) with "Black."

The movement generated a number of positive developments. Probably the most noteworthy of these was its influence on Black culture. For the first time, Blacks in the United States were encouraged to acknowledge their African heritage. Colleges and universities established Black studies programs and departments. Blacks who had grown up believing that they were descended from a backwards people now found out that African culture was as rich and diverse as any other, and they were encouraged to take pride in that heritage. The Black arts movement, seen by some as connected to the Black Power movement, flourished in the 1960s and 1970s. Young

---

8. Staffan Müller-Wille, "Linnaeus and the Four Corners of the World," in *The Cultural Politics of Blood, 1500-1900*, ed. Kimberly Anne Coles et al. (London: Palgrave Macmillan, 2015).

Black poets, authors, and visual artists found their voices and shared those voices with others. Unlike earlier Black arts movements such as the Harlem Renaissance, the new movement primarily sought out a Black audience.

I'll take my seat when I tell you this: God also loves Black people. You have to get this—I said God loves Black people.

In the Amos text, we are reminded that the God of the universe in not limited to just the Israelites. The overall and surely indisputable message is that God has created us all in his image and has included all members of the human race in the saving work of his Son.

Nowhere does the Bible give any indications that Black people or any people, whether "of color" or not, are outside the embrace of his love. But the fact remains that people have believed and taught this error, and sadly, it has been a teaching that still affects the way many of us think about each other, and perhaps even ourselves.

The Bible does not focus on skin color as any form of criterion. All have sinned, all have fallen short of the glory of God, and all are recipients of his grace through Jesus Christ.

God says, "Am I not involved with all nations? Didn't I bring Israel up from Egypt, the Philistines from Caphtor, the Arameans from Qir? But you can be sure that I, God, the Master, have my eye on the Kingdom of Sin."

What is clear from this passage in Amos is that God is aware of the Blacks in the Bible that undoubtedly existed and played significant roles in biblical history of redemption.

Women and men of all colors must know that they are made in God's image, that Jesus Christ died to redeem them, and that if they believe, he will be theirs and they will be his.

Like Hagar, we need to know that God is ever-ready to hear.

Like Zipporah, we need to use all our gifts and knowledge of survival to help others.

Like Jethro, we need to use our gifts of teaching and administration.

Like Hobab, we need to be willing to help guide those in need.

Like the Queen of Sheba, we need to enlarge and better our minds and souls.

Like the beautiful Black women of the Song of Songs, we need to love chastely with all-out commitment to our beloved.

Like the Ethiopian high official, we need to seek above all for God's truth and be ready to accept and act upon the answers God will provide those who seek him.

Like the men and women of Antioch, we need to go and give and pray. We all need to be a transforming influence for Jesus Christ.

Black is blessed, and may God make the world ready to receive this blessing. So call me Black. I don't have a problem with that!

Chapter 3
Hollywood and Films Have Not Gotten It Right

"They killed this dude name Jesus. ...
What do you think they'll do to you?"
—Jamie Foxx, They Cloned Tyrone [1]

"Excuse me, kind sir, if you could point me to the elevator
that leads to the freaky laboratory, I'll be out your atmosphere."
—Jamie Foxx, They Cloned Tyrone

"When we watch ourselves on screen being heroic, or desired, or brilliant,
or in love, we can see that for ourselves. And the world sees that in us."
—Gina Prince-Bythewood, director [2]

Sermon Site Media Tag: Black Jesus in the Movie 'Red Tails'
Contributed by Amiri Hooker, January 2, 2014
6,608 views before rejection
Scripture: Revelation 1:14-15
Denomination: United Methodist

About the sermon:

This sermon was written in response to a popular movie, *Red Tails*, about the Tuskegee Airmen, the first African-American military aviators in the United States

---

1. Juel Taylor, dir., *They Cloned Tyrone*, Netflix, 2023.

2. Gina Prince-Bythewood, "Director Gina Prince-Bythewood: Representation Still Too Rare in Hollywood (Guest Column)," *Variety*, February 27, 2020, https://variety.com/2020/artisans/opinion/black-history-month-director-gina-prince-bythewood-1203517648/.

Armed Forces. I enjoy watching movies and believe sermons connect better when they are based on a popular song, film, play, or event. The United States of America is a country known for its diverse tapestry of religions and faith traditions. From the earliest days of its founding, religion has played a pivotal role in shaping American society, culture, and values. Throughout history, religion has also played a significant role in shaping the American identity. From the "city upon a hill" metaphor in the Puritan settlement to Martin Luther King Jr.'s advocacy for civil rights based on Christian principles, faith has been intertwined with notions of morality, justice, and the pursuit of a more perfect union.

The intertwining of Hollywood and religion in America is a fascinating phenomenon that has shaped the nation's cultural landscape for more than a century. From the early days of silent cinema to the modern blockbuster era, the silver screen has reflected and influenced religious beliefs, values, and practices. Religious themes have been recurrent on the silver screen throughout Hollywood's history. From biblical epics such as *The Ten Commandments* (1956) and *Ben-Hur* (1959) to contemporary films such as *The Passion of the Christ* (2004) and *Noah* (2014), religious narratives have captivated audiences and sparked discussions about faith and spirituality. Religion often tackles questions of morality and ethical dilemmas, and so does Hollywood. Films frequently explore complex moral issues, challenging audiences to reflect on their values and beliefs. This intersection between entertainment and ethical exploration has spurred debates on societal norms and the role of religion in shaping them.

Excerpt of rejection:
"Hi again, Amiri, with other sermons about claiming that Jesus is Black, this sermon, too, cannot stand."

Reflection:
The color of Jesus is one of the themes we see repeatedly in movies and films. As America's religious landscape continues to evolve, the relationship between Hollywood and religion will likely continue to shape and be shaped by the nation's cultural fabric. Through responsible storytelling and thoughtful representations, the film industry has the power to foster understanding, empathy, and dialogue, making the connection between Hollywood and religion a vital aspect of American popular culture.

The portrayal of Jesus Christ as a Black man in movies and films has been a source of controversy and celebration. Filmmakers have grappled with the concept of Black Jesus, challenging traditional representations of the revered religious figure. The concept of Black Jesus in film draws inspiration from historical evidence suggesting that Jesus Christ was likely of Middle Eastern descent with dark skin. However, traditional Western art and media portrayals have often depicted him as a White man. The shift toward representing Jesus as Black in films aims to challenge the Eurocentric perspective and provide a more historically accurate portrayal.

In the genre of biblical epics, which has been a mainstay in cinema, filmmakers have sought to offer diverse perspectives on Jesus's life and teachings. Movies such as *The Greatest Story Ever Told* (1965) and *Son of Man* (2006) present compelling depictions of a Black Jesus, sparking conversations about the importance of inclusive representation. For many Black viewers, seeing Jesus portrayed as one of their own in movies can be empowering and validating. Such depictions offer a sense of belonging and recognition in a society where representations of religious figures have often excluded non-White perspectives.

What Jesus looked like has long been debated by theologians around the world. Different cultures have imagined him in different ways, says Stephen Prothero, chairman of the religion department at Boston University. In Japan, Jesus looks Japanese. In Africa, he is Black. But in America, he is almost always White, like the fair-haired savior painted by Leonardo Da Vinci in *The Last Supper* in 1495. While some Black churches have images of a Black Jesus behind the altar and others have claimed Christ was Black, Prothero says, "none of those arguments or images have filtered much into the mainstream."[3] "Black people in this country are the only race of people who worship a god outside their own image," says filmmaker Jean-Claude La Marre, adding that showing Christ as a Black man is "the most poignant way to deal with the issue of race in this country because it goes to the heart of how we look at the world."[4]

Seeing Christ as Black also provides a positive image of Blacks, something that's been scant in the United States, says the Rev. Cecil "Chip" Murray, longtime leader of Los Angeles's First African Methodist Episcopal Church and a producer of the film *Color of the Cross* (2006). The most important theological image in the White male supremacy system is that of White Jesus. By supremacists' perverted logic, if the White race is the "master race," then the world's savior has to be a White man. If the Son of God is White, then God must be White.[5] The entire theology of White male supremacy revolves around the whiteness of Jesus. If Jesus's whiteness were eliminated, the theological foundation of the White male supremacy system would be threatened.

To me, this notion was expressed most profoundly in an episode in the 1970s

---

3. Stephenson Humphries-Brooks, *Cinematic Savior: Hollywood's Making of the American Christ* (Westport, Conn.: Praeger, 2006).

4. Sandy Cohen, "New Movie Shows Jesus as Black," October 25, 2006, https://www.cbsnews.com/news/new-movie-shows-jesus-as-black.

5. Theron D. Williams, *The Bible Is Black History* (Indianapolis, IN: The Bible is Black History Institute, 2020).

sitcom *Good Times*. This weekly situation comedy was about a struggling African-American family that lived in a Chicago public housing project. It aired on the CBS television network from 1974 to 1979. The parents, James and Florida Evans, did their best to raise their three children to be decent human beings in spite of their impoverished living conditions. The sitcom's inaugural season aired an episode titled "Black Jesus." The precocious youngest son of the family, Michael, while rummaging through the personal effects of his older brother, J.J. (a naturally talented artist), came across a portrait J.J. had painted of Black Jesus. Michael, whose social consciousness far exceeded his age, removed from the wall the picture of White Jesus—to which Mrs. Evans would often pray—and replaced it with J.J.'s rendition of Black Jesus. Despite the good fortune that this struggling family experienced while Black Jesus hung on the wall, Mrs. Evans was determined not to allow Black Jesus to usurp White Jesus's position in the Evans household. I can't tell you how many times I watched this episode growing up and how many times I wanted to take down my grandmother's White Jesus and replace it.

In turn, this sermon replaced the many times I have wanted to replace the notion of White supremacy in sermons and church.

In a time when racial struggles defined a generation, the movie *Red Tails* emerged as a beacon of hope, showcasing the inspiring true story of the Tuskegee Airmen—the first African-American pilots in the United States military. Directed by Anthony Hemingway and produced by George Lucas, this film stands as a testament to the indomitable human spirit and the power of unity. *Red Tails* transports audiences to the 1940s, a period when racism and prejudice were rampant in the U.S. Armed Forces. Despite facing systemic discrimination, the Tuskegee Airmen, portrayed masterfully by a talented ensemble cast, refuse to be deterred by adversity. Instead, they band together, harnessing their exceptional skills and determination to prove their worth and contribute valiantly to their country. The film captivates viewers with stunning aerial sequences that leave them on the edge of their seats. The special effects and cinematography combine to create a gripping experience, enabling audiences to grasp the heroism and sacrifice of these pioneering aviators truly. The dedication and camaraderie displayed on screen transcend race, reminding us of the universal strength of working together toward a common goal.

At its core, *Red Tails* celebrates the human spirit's triumph over prejudice. By highlighting the airmen's unwavering commitment to their duty and their country, the movie transcends the confines of history, offering a timeless message of resilience and hope. It encourages viewers to confront the past and reflect on the progress made while acknowledging the work that still remains to be done in the fight for equality and justice. Yes, there was a debate about the color of Jesus in the film. But this was a very small section of the film and should not overshadow a great attempt at capturing a part of the African-American legacy in this country.

The film's powerful narrative also serves as a poignant reminder of the importance of representation in cinema. *Red Tails* sheds light on a relatively unknown chapter in history and gives a long-overdue platform to the Tuskegee Airmen and their incredible contributions. By elevating these heroes to the silver screen, the movie champions the idea that every community's story deserves to be shared and celebrated.

The Banned Sermon:
Black Jesus in the Movie 'Red Tails'
By Amiri Hooker, January 2, 2014
Scripture: Revelation 1:14-15
Denomination: United Methodist

Scripture text:

Revelation 1:14-15 (NIV), "The hair on his head was white like wool, as white as snow, and his eyes were like blazing fire. His feet were like bronze glowing in a furnace, and his voice was like the sound of rushing waters."

Introduction:

This sermon looks at race and class and the historical Jesus. This sermon looks at new and old film trends and Jesus the Christ in the African-American community. This sermon also looks at a new Barbie doll from the BK Label.

Main body:

Red Tails the movie is a great film. The movie tells the story of World War II and how a group of professional and outstanding pilots changed persons' respect for Black pilots and changed the nature of the war. In 1925, a U.S. War Department study of African Americans' participation in World War I deemed Black soldiers "inferior" and "cowards," untrustworthy in the heat of battle.

Two decades later, however, that prejudiced assessment would be roundly rebuked by the courage and flying finesse of an all-Black group of pilots known as the Tuskegee Airmen.

Before these flyers could fully join the fray in the skies above Europe, however, they would first have to win another battle back home—the battle against an establishment still entrenched in the conviction that Black pilots were bad pilots.

Red Tails relays the essence of their true story, with fictionalized characters standing in for historical ones.

It's 1944, two years after the Army officially launched its experimental pilot training program for Black soldiers in Tuskegee, Alabama. Graduates of that program, the pilots and ground crew of the 332nd Fighter Group, are biding their time at Ramitelli Airfield in Italy. The unit sees regular action piloting dilapidated P-40 fighters to raid German trains and convoys. But that's nothing compared to the real combat happening one hundred miles to the north.

Several pilots are Christians who believe prayer is key to staying safe in combat. One is a pilot with the call sign Deke—short for Deacon—who carries a picture of an African-American savior whom he affectionately calls "Black Jesus."

At one point, he prays, "Black Jesus, we thank you for bringing Red Squadron home."

A spirited conversation between Deke and Joker (who often wins at poker) revolves around whether God protects pilots in battle or whether they're just lucky. Deke insists that prayer makes a difference, while Joker is agnostic on that front.

A chaplain prays for the squadron's protection, ending his intercession in Jesus's name. An officer gives a speech saying God is on the Red Tails' side.

Point 1: Jesus is on our side

This idea of Jesus protecting folks as they go off to do battle is nothing new; Christians believe in their heart when they go to do something valuable, something important, that God, Jesus, and the Holy Spirit go with them.

One of the unique things about us is that we don't have a problem taking Jesus with us wherever we go.

"Later, Jesus showed himself to two of his followers while they were walking in the country, but he did not look the same as before" (Mark 16:12 NCV).

I don't have a problem with that because I understand that no matter how the historic Jesus looked in the past resurrection, Jesus looked different. If you don't know your Bible, you will argue not over how the historic Jesus must have looked. While I am sure that Jesus of Nazareth had a certain appearance, I also know that the after-resurrection Jesus Christ is described in Revelation: "The hair on his head was white like wool, as white as snow, and his eyes were like blazing fire. His feet were like bronze glowing in a furnace, and his voice was like the sound of rushing waters" (Revelation 1:14-15 NIV).

So no matter how others might want to debate how Jesus looked, no one can debate that Christ looked very much like most of us regarding Scripture.

An illustration: A little girl is asked to do a Black history report, and the teacher makes the mistake of asking her to write about the most important Black historic figure she can thank. She starts going through the list of the fab five and the big ten.

She says, "These were all nice, but I really want a good grade, so who was the greatest figure in all of recorded history that was also by gifted of God to be Black like me?"

After a few more minutes, she came up with the name—Jesus.

Jesus who also, according to the book, at which every head shall bow, and every tongue shall confess.

Point 2: Black Jesus in films is nothing new

I discovered some years ago, with the help of some of my mentors, that Spike Lee uses Jesus images in his movie, and at the point of rising conflict you can find these on a wall, side table, keychain, or some other place in the movie.

Filmmaker Jean-Claude La Marre says he wrote *Color of the Cross* because "Black people in this country are the only race of people who worship a God outside their own image."

However, one of the things I appreciated about Red Tails is that this concept was highlighted but never seemed to be forced, and the movie even had a debate as to whether Jesus is even listening or not.

That helped me understand the pain that Jesus Christ's followers are able to endure.

Point 3: Understanding Jesus as Black is hard for some of us

Many of us have an issue with the concept of Jesus as Black because we have an issue with blackness. Yes, the idea of Black is bad. Black is evil; Black is ugly. The darker something is, the worse it is.

Illustration: My daughter received a doll this year—a Black Barbie. She is Black, a very beautiful, very dark doll. I had to talk to the doll for a few days. I looked at this very African-looking doll with her hard features and long looks.

I said, "Do you realize you are different from the dolls little girls normally get? Do you realize I have never seen anything like you? Do you realize that while I understand that you are beautiful, your beauty scares me? It's not the normal milk chocolate; you are very dark and very beautiful. Little doll, I give you the permission to be Black and beautiful."

The doll kind of looked at me and said, "Rev, I give you the permission to be Black and beautiful."

And then it hit me as if Jesus had been walking with me on the road of Damascus and asking questions all day.

Conclusion: And I say, Jesus, I give you my permission to be Black and beautiful.

And it's as if Jesus looks back at me and says, "Do I need to walk you through all the prophecy dealing with me in the Bible? I don't need your permission; I am who I am. I am what my father made me be, and I don't need your permission after coming through the fire. I have been polished and have been transformed into the resurrected Lord. And have no problems being Black and dark and beautiful because that is who God made me to be. But I give you permission, Rev, to be Black and see it as beautiful, because that is how God made you."

Chapter 4
Higher Education and the Miseducation of the Church Negro

"As another has well said, to handicap a student by teaching him that his Black face is a curse and that his struggle to change his condition is hopeless is the worst sort of lynching."—Carter Woodson, The Mis-Education of the Negro [1]

"We are a city that has had Islam for one thousand years. We had the greatest teachers and universities. And now these Bedouins, these illiterates, these ignoramuses, tell us how to wear our pants, and how to say our prayers, and how our wives should dress, as if they were the ones who invented the way?"
—Joshua Hammer, The Bad-Ass Librarians of Timbuktu and Their Race to Save the World's Most Precious Manuscripts [2]

Sermon Site Tag: The Best Schools Are In Egypt
Contributed by Amiri Hooker, January 2, 2014
7,083 views before rejection
Scripture: Matthew 2:13-23
Denomination: United Methodist

About the sermon:

This sermon was an attempt to look at higher education and Carter G. Woodson's concept of miseducation as a way of disproving Christianity as a purely White man's

---

1. Carter Godwin Woodson, *The Mis-Education of the Negro* (London: Penguin Classics, 2023).
2. Joshua Hammer, *The Bad-Ass Librarians of Timbuktu: And Their Race to Save the World's Most Precious Manuscripts* (New York: Simon and Schuster, 2016).

religion. The perception that Christianity is exclusively a "White man's religion" is a narrative that has persisted for far too long, overshadowing the global diversity and inclusivity of the faith. It was my hope that shedding light on the rich and diverse history of Christianity might provide insights, emphasizing the global nature of the Christian faith and debunking the notion that it is limited to any particular race or culture. I also hoped to highlight at some juncture the importance of early childhood development and control over the institutional biases we discover in looking at Greek and Roman traditions as superior to other traditions.

This sermon should also edify that a significant aspect of Christianity's global presence is its deep-rooted history in Africa. The early African Christian communities, like the Coptic Christians in Egypt, played a vital role in shaping Christian theology and preserving the faith's teachings. One must also acknowledge that early African education/schools had a real historical role in the creation of Western schools, i.e., Western religion. The traditional concept of Western supremacy in the education narrative often overlooks the substantial African contributions to the development of Western knowledge and civilization.

Excerpt of rejection:

"Hi, Amiri, The sermon is being rejected for the following reasons. Jesus, his family, his disciples and, doubtless, most of the fellow Jews he encountered in his public ministry were persons of color. They would certainly not be Europeans. They were individuals from the region of Palestine under Roman rule. ... Matthew 2:13-15 gives us the reason Jesus's family fled to Egypt. ... To understand this text referring to race is to read something into the text that is not there. ...The origin of people began in the Garden of Eden located somewhere in Asia (north of Israel to the Black Sea or east of Israel near the Persian Gulf). This is where all humanity descends from (Adam) according to Scripture."

Reflection:

Africa is widely acknowledged as the birthplace of the human race and has contributed much to shaping the Christian mind.[3] The thinking of Augustine of Hippo (354-430), an African, has shaped Christian doctrine and theology for centuries and is still influential today. In the centuries before Augustine, hundreds of African martyrs died for their faith, with their shed blood as the seed for the spread of Christianity in Europe. African desert monks pioneered the monastic system that preserved the Holy Scriptures in turbulent times and laid the foundations for Western civilization.

---

3. Thomas C. Oden, *How Africa Shaped the Christian Mind: Rediscovering the African Seedbed of Western Christianity* (Westmont, Ill.: Intervarsity Press, 2010).

The intellectual achievements of ancient African universities—Timbuktu, Alexandria, Al Quaraouiyine, Sijilmasa, Cairo, Gao, and others—testify to the continent's vibrant tradition of higher education and cultural exchange. These great centers of learning attracted scholars from diverse regions and contributed significantly to advancing knowledge, philosophy, theology, and science. These ancient African universities were not just learning centers but also cultural exchange hubs. Scholars from different regions and backgrounds interacted, enriching their knowledge and understanding of various cultures. The impact of these institutions on knowledge dissemination and cultural integration extended far beyond Africa's borders.

By embracing the legacy of these ancient universities, we acknowledge Africa's profound impact on the global history of scholarship and culture. It is essential to recognize and celebrate the intellectual achievements of these institutions as they continue to inspire and inform the world today.

The Library of Alexandria, one of the most renowned centers of learning in the ancient world, stood on the African continent in Egypt. This library attracted scholars and intellectuals from various cultures, including Greek thinkers such as Euclid and Archimedes. The library's vast collection of texts and manuscripts was a hub of knowledge fostering cross-cultural exchanges. Carter G. Woodson argued that Greek philosophy, including the works of Plato and Aristotle, bore the marks of African influence. He highlighted the travels of Pythagoras to Egypt, where he studied the wisdom of Egyptian priests. The philosophical concepts of mathematics, ethics, and metaphysics are believed to have drawn inspiration from African teachings.

This concept of stolen legacy is one of the main reasons so many churchgoers have no idea about the true origins of Kemetic teachings. Historical evidence suggests that ancient Greece maintained extensive interactions with Africa, particularly through trade, migration, and cultural exchange. The Nile River Valley civilizations, such as Egypt and Nubia, were well-established centers of knowledge and advanced cultures that significantly influenced the ancient world. Vince L. Bantu's perspective provides crucial insights into the African contributions to ancient Greek knowledge, challenging the prevailing narrative that overlooks these valuable connections.[4] The evidence of cultural exchange, intellectual influences, and adaptability highlights the symbiotic relationship between Africa and ancient Greece. Embracing a more comprehensive view of history enables us to appreciate the interconnectedness of human civilizations and celebrate the diverse heritage that shaped the world's cultural and intellectual tapestry. By acknowledging the African influence on ancient Greece, we honor the legacy of knowledge and wisdom shared between these two great civilizations.

During the Persian, Greek, and Roman invasions, large numbers of Egyptians

---

4. Vince L. Bantu, *A Multitude of All Peoples: Engaging Ancient Christianity's Global Identity* (Downers Grove, Ill.: IVP Academic, 2020), Kindle.

fled not only to the desert and mountain regions but also to adjacent lands in Africa, Arabia, and Asia Minor, where they lived and secretly developed the teachings that belonged to their mystery system. In the eighth century the Moors, i.e., natives of Mauritania in North Africa, invaded Spain and took with them the Egyptian culture they had preserved.

Knowledge in the ancient days was centralized, i.e., it belonged to a common parent and system, i.e., the wisdom teaching or mysteries of Egypt, which the Greeks used to call Sophia. The wisdom spoken of in the biblical text and the biblical tradition is indeed the fountain of wisdom and understanding that came from the schools in Egypt. During their occupation of Spain the Moors displayed, with considerable credit, the grandeur of African culture and civilization. The schools and libraries they established became famous throughout the medieval world; science and learning were cultivated and taught. The schools of Cordova, Toledo, Seville, and Saragossa attained such celebrity that they, like their parent Egypt, attracted students from all parts of the Western world.

And from them arose the most famous African professors the world has ever known in medicine, surgery, astronomy, and mathematics. But these people from North Africa did more than merely distinguish themselves in Spain. They were really the recognized custodians of African culture, to whom the world looked for enlightenment. Consequently, philosophy and the various branches of science were disseminated through the medium of the ancient Arabic language.

Education in ancient civilizations played a pivotal role in shaping the societies they existed in, and ancient Egypt was no exception. During the time of Jesus, which corresponds roughly to the period of 4 B.C. to A.D. 30, Egypt was a center of cultural and intellectual exchange, and education held great importance in the lives of its people. Education was primarily imparted through temple schools, which were often attached to prominent religious establishments. These schools were exclusive and usually reserved for the children of priests, scribes, and the elite class. The curriculum focused on religious studies, hieroglyphics, mathematics, and the art of writing. During the time of Jesus, Egypt was a hub of cultural exchange and attracted scholars, philosophers, and intellectuals from across the Mediterranean and beyond. This interaction facilitated sharing of knowledge, ideas, and innovations, contributing to the flourishing of arts, sciences, and religious practices in Egypt.

The life of Jesus Christ remains an intriguing subject of historical and theological exploration. While much is known about his adult ministry, there are gaps in our understanding of his early years. One of the most debated aspects is whether Jesus was taught in Egyptian schools during his childhood. This sheds light on this enigmatic question and examines the historical evidence surrounding this theory.

The New Testament's Gospel of Matthew accounts for Joseph, Mary, and the infant Jesus fleeing to Egypt to escape King Herod's wrath. According to the Gospel, they remained in Egypt until it was safe to return to their homeland. This "Flight to Egypt" narrative has led some scholars to speculate that Jesus was exposed to the renowned educational system of Egypt during this period.

The Banned Sermon:
The Best Schools Are in Egypt
Contributed by Amiri Hooker, January 2, 2014
Scripture: Matthew 2:13-23
Denomination: United Methodist

Scripture text:
Matthew 2:13-15 (NIV), "When they had gone, an angel of the Lord appeared to Joseph in a dream. 'Get up,' he said, 'take the child and his mother and escape to Egypt. Stay there until I tell you, for Herod is going to search for the child to kill him.' So he got up, took the child and his mother during the night and left for Egypt, where he stayed until the death of Herod. And so was fulfilled what the Lord had said through the prophet: 'Out of Egypt I called my son.'"

Introduction:
This is a sermon about the time Jesus spent in Egypt and the ideals Jesus may have developed while in living in the Coptic presences. The sermon looks at some basic concepts that young men need to develop.

Main body:
Many kindred souls lived in Egypt at the time, and Mary, Joseph, and Jesus would have easily found refuge there. Matthew tells us only that the holy family stayed in Egypt "until the death of Herod," an unspecified length of time. But a number of apocryphal tales fill in the details. These stories are especially important to the Egyptian Coptic Church, which states that the holy family remained in Egypt for a little over three and a half years.

Unfortunately, the U.S. will never boast a medieval university, as this country's origins, established in 1776 with the Declaration of Independence, were formed when the oldest university in the world was about nine centuries old.

However, the university as an autonomous self-governing institution first was developed as religious institutions (madrasahs) that originated in the medieval Islamic world. Al-Azhar University, located in Egypt, is the world's second-oldest surviving degree-granting institute. Founded in 970-972, this university serves as a center for

Arabic literature and Sunni Islamic learning. Al-Azhar University concentrates upon a religious syllabus, which pays special attention to the Quranic sciences and traditions of the Prophet Muhammad on the one hand, while also teaching all modern fields of science. Yet this was a combination of many older schools all over Egypt.

In the Gospel of Matthew, we find the quotation from Hosea 11:1, which reads, "Out of Egypt I called my son." The passage is part of the notorious "Flight into Egypt." If the holy family were indeed persons who looked like typical "Europeans," could they effectively "hide" in Africa? No. One must remember and take most seriously the fact that Egypt has always been and remains part of Africa. Her indigenous people are noticeably different from the European.

Jesus, his family, his disciples and, doubtless, most of the fellow Jews he encountered in his public ministry, were persons of color. They would certainly not be Europeans. Matthew makes sure to point this out.

In Matthew 1:1-14 we also have the genealogy of Jesus, in which four Afro-Asiatic women are included: Rahab, Tamar, Ruth, and Bathsheba.

You see today in our text Matthew 2:13-18, "Out of Egypt (Africa) I called my son" (see Hosea 11:1).

And even later in the text, Matthew 12:42, it talks about "The Queen of the South," meaning "the Queen of Sheba" (parallel reference in Luke 11:31; compare 1 Kings 10:1-10 and 2 Chronicles 9:1-9).

In Matthew 27:32, we're told Simon of Cyrene was compelled to carry the cross (parallel accounts in Mark 15:21 and Luke 23:26).

So I wonder: What would a young Jesus need to learn in Egypt about being Black that would help him in life?

An illustration: Let me see if I can set this up. There was a plane crash up north in the mountains somewhere, and when the rescuers found the victims they were brokenhearted because they discovered a little boy that had died. They realized that the crash had not killed him but that he had died from starvation. That's what made this even more traumatic—he had died not from the impact of the crash, but he died from starvation … and only feet away were dried food and bottled water. Get this. He died not from the impact of the crash, but he died in a real sense from not knowing what he had going on for him. If only he had known what he had going for him, he would have survived the crash.

Beloved, the angel of God told Joseph to take his son to Egypt because he needed to understand what he was working with. There was some freezer dried knowledge and some water of the Nile that Jesus needed to fully understand how to live as an oppressed targeted minority in Herod's world.

So here are six things that every Black boy, needs to know as we are in the middle of Kwanzaa. We also speak now to the generations of our sons that are as yet unborn.

This is our message to you:

1. You come from greatness. Just because one is born into a disadvantaged household, neighborhood, or upbringing doesn't necessarily mean that it therefore has to be born in him.

2. Respect and protect the Black women. That is, those that respect themselves. Respect has to be earned, individual by individual, and each entirely of his or her own accord. The Black woman is, however, the queen and the precious jewel that God has so graciously seen fit to bless us, of all men, with—with a dignified, respectable sister behind and beside you.

3. Whatever you become, you were Black first. Whatever you prepare yourself for—a career as a doctor, a lawyer, an engineer, or a plumber—this society will always view you as a Black doctor, a Black lawyer, a Black engineer, and so on. Get used to the idea, and choose to wear it, as well as your passion for excellence, like a badge of honor. Have no tolerance for mediocrity.

4. Always project and carry yourself with dignity. You are the son of the original people of the earth, and of the great kings and princes of Africa. Walk with your head up, render a firm handshake, and look anyone, White or Black, directly in the eye when you speak to them. Be true to your word when you give it to someone, and make it mean something.

5. The world and society owe you nothing. It has been said, "You may not get all you pay for in life, but you'll certainly pay for all you get." No one owes you a scholarship simply because you've earned good grades, and nobody owes you a job once you've been awarded a degree or mastered a certain skill. If you want something, anything at all, you have to go out and get it. No more, and no less.

6. No one is successful by accident. You must plan your work and work your plan, young man. People who are successful are the ones least surprised by it when they attain it, because they likely have been working toward their dreams and ambitions all along. It's just everyone else around them (and who usually doubted or tried to discourage them) who begins to behave differently. Don't blindly buy into what someone else determines it to be, though. Define and decide what success means to you, and then achieve it on your own terms.

These are Black things that you must understand.

Peace and strength.

Chapter 5
Who Has the Rock Next?

"During times of war, hatred becomes quite respectable, even though it has to masquerade often under the guise of patriotism."—Howard Thurman [1]

"It is ironic that America, with its history of injustice to the poor, especially the Black man and the Indian, prides itself on being a Christian nation."—James H. Cone [2]

"But race is the child of racism, not the father."
—*Ta-Nehisi Coates,* Between the World and Me [3]

Sermon Site Mega Tag: The Jesus-Rock Issue: Four of the Seven
Last Words on the Cross
By Amiri Hooker, April 7, 2015
12,319 views before rejection
Scripture: Psalms 22:1-2
Denomination: United Methodist

About the sermon:
   This was a sermonette written for a seasonal service during Lent. There is a great tradition in the church that during Lent/Easter, the Black church hosts a service on Good Friday. The program is a major celebration of preaching called the "Seven Last Words" or "Seven Last Saying from the Cross." This worship service is nor-

---

1. Howard Thurman, *Jesus and the Disinherited* (Boston: Beacon Press, 2012).
2. James H. Cone, *Black Theology and Black Power* (Maryknoll, NY: Orbis Books, 1997).
3. Ta-Nehisi Coates, *Between the World and Me* (London: One World, 2015).

mally done with a collection of seven speakers who each have five to ten minutes to expound on one of the last sayings of Jesus from the cross.

The fourth saying or word is the central focus of this sermonette and deals with abandonment. In this brief sermon, there was a desire to connect that notion of Jesus's cup of all salvation and loneliness with the feeling of abandonment Black and former slaves must have experienced during the time of lynchings in the antebellum and reconstruction South. One should also note the meaning of the term "rock." In basketball, the term "the rock" is a colloquial expression used to refer to the basketball itself. It is a slang term commonly used by players, coaches, and fans as a way of talking about the ball during a game or when discussing basketball-related topics. The term highlights the central role of basketball in the sport, as it is the object that players must pass, dribble, and shoot to score points and win the game. Thus, referring to Jesus as the rock also points to his centrality and connection to the Black community.

Excerpt of rejection:

"There is only one statement you made here that I am struggling to understand. You stated, 'What does it mean that God would let Jesus his only son feel the pain of the cross? The pain of being lynched as Black male in public.' Can you please flesh out a bit of what you mean here and resubmit it to clear up any confusion? It appears that you're saying Jesus was lynched as a Black male in public, but I'm not quite certain if that is in fact what you are saying. Or perhaps you're connecting it to the pain a Black male would feel if he were to be lynched in public. Please help our readers understand what you are saying better."

Reflections:

At the heart of Black preaching lies the recognition of the profound suffering experienced by Black individuals throughout history. From the brutalities of slavery to the injustices of systemic racism, the African-American community has faced adversity at every turn. James Cone, a pioneer in Black liberation theology, asserted that preaching must echo the cries of the oppressed, vocalizing their pain and striving for justice and equality. Black preaching serves as an avenue to reconcile the enduring tension between the Black experience and the Christian faith. Cone reminds us that the Gospel of Jesus Christ is not a mere abstraction but a lived reality that directly confronts the struggles of the oppressed. It must engage with the concrete realities of life in the margins, empowering the marginalized to envision a world where their dignity and humanity are affirmed.

In today's society, the need for Black preaching is as urgent as ever. While progress has been made, systemic racism continues to perpetuate inequalities in various spheres of life.

Black preachers have a responsibility to call out these injustices fearlessly and advocate for transformative change. Additionally, Black preaching must engage in constructive dialogue with other faith traditions, seeking to build bridges and unite communities in the pursuit of justice. Cone reminds us that solidarity across diverse groups is essential for dismantling the structures of oppression and advancing the cause of liberation.

Within the Black community, sermons serve as sources of healing and empowerment. Samuel Proctor's teachings often emphasized the importance of lifting up the marginalized and healing the wounds of the oppressed. Black preachers today must continue this tradition, providing hope and strength to those who face adversity.

In this contemplative mini sermon, we delve into the profound parallels between the suffering endured on the cross and the harrowing pain of the lynching tree. Embracing the perspectives of the late James Cone, a trailblazing theologian, we explore how these historical symbols of brutality intersect to illuminate the shared agony of marginalized communities.

The crucifixion of Jesus Christ and the lynching of African Americans symbolize the grotesque manifestations of hatred, racism, and dehumanization, revealing the necessity for collective healing and solidarity. The cross, a symbol of Christianity, stands as a representation of the crucifixion of Jesus Christ, while the lynching tree embodies the horrors of racial violence and discrimination against African Americans. Both events have left a profound impact on humanity, marking the struggles faced by oppressed communities throughout history. At the heart of these interconnected narratives lies the notion of suffering and sacrifice. Jesus Christ's crucifixion served as a sacrificial act, symbolizing redemption and salvation. Similarly, the lynching tree became a sacrificial site where innocent lives were unjustly taken, reflecting a dark chapter in American history.

The cross and the lynching tree both exemplify the dehumanization and marginalization faced by their respective communities. Jesus, an innocent man, was subject to humiliation and pain, mirroring the experiences of African Americans who were treated as subhuman during the era of lynching. Cone's liberation theology offers a profound insight into the connection between these two symbols of pain. He believed that the Gospel of Jesus Christ was inseparable from the liberation of the oppressed, encouraging a radical commitment to justice, equality, and compassion. The pain inflicted on the cross and the lynching tree continues to reverberate through history, impacting the collective memory of communities affected by such atrocities. To foster healing and reconciliation, we must acknowledge these past injustices and engage in open dialogue, promoting empathy and understanding.

The Black song tradition has a rich history deeply rooted in the African-American

experience, reflecting the struggles, joys, and faith of the community. Modern Gospel singers, such as Kirk Franklin and others, have played a pivotal role in redefining this tradition, infusing it with contemporary styles and messages. However, the question arises: Do these artists take the pain out of the Black gospel tradition?

Gospel music has evolved over time, reflecting the changing cultural landscape and musical trends. While traditional gospel music often expressed the pain and hardships faced by African Americans, modern gospel singers such as Kirk Franklin have adopted a more diverse musical palette, incorporating elements of R&B, hip-hop, and contemporary pop. Recently, the rise of popular hits such as "Jesus Rock" and "Jesus Walk" has sparked debates within the Christian community about whether these songs reflect a lack of respect for faith. "Jesus Rock" and "Jesus Walk" may explore a wider range of spiritual themes beyond traditional gospel music's typical repertoire. While some purists may argue that these songs deviate from the core gospel message, others see them as an opportunity to delve into social justice, personal struggles, and modern-day challenges faced by believers. These songs signify a broader cultural shift within the Christian community, seeking to engage diverse audiences through various musical styles and themes.

Rather than a lack of respect for faith, these songs represent a fresh and authentic expression of spirituality if the writers are sincere in their faith expression.

The Banned Sermon:
The Jesus-Rock Issue: Four of the Seven Last Words on the Cross
By Amiri Hooker, April 7, 2015
Scripture: Psalms 22:1-2
Denomination: United Methodist

Scripture text:
Psalm 22:1-2 (NLT), "My God, my God, why have you abandoned me? Why are you so far away when I groan for help? Every day I call to you, my God, but you do not answer. Every night I lift my voice, but I find no relief."

Introduction:
This sermon looks at what it means that God would let Jesus his only son feel the pain of the cross, the pain of being lynched as Black male figure in public, and how that pain has been whitewashed in our community these days. (Very short sermon: 7 minutes.)

As Jesus was dying on the cross, he quoted the scripture he echoed at the beginning of Psalm 22, which reads, "My God, my God, why have you abandoned me?

Why are you so far away when I groan for help? Every day I call to you, my God, but you do not answer. Every night you hear my voice, but I find no relief" (v. 1-2 NLT).

Or in The Message Bible, as Eugene Peterson says it, "God, God . . . my God! Why did you dump me miles from nowhere? Doubled up with pain, I call to God all the day long. No answer. Nothing. I keep at it all night, tossing and turning."

Main sermon:

In the words of the psalmist, Jesus found a way to express the cry of his heart: Why had God abandoned him? Why did his father turn his back on Jesus in his moment of greatest agony? Why did God dump on me? As Martin Luther once said, "God forsaking God. Who can understand it?"

The cross has been transformed into a harmless, non-offensive ornament that Christians wear around their necks. Rather than reminding us of the "cost of discipleship," it has become a form of "cheap grace," an easy way to salvation that doesn't force us to confront the power of Christ's message and mission until we can see the cross and the lynching tree together."[4]

What we do know is that Jesus on the cross entered into the hell of separation from God.

The Father abandoned him because Jesus took upon himself the penalty for our sins. In that excruciating moment, he experienced something far more horrible than physical pain.

The beloved Son of God knew what it was like to be rejected by the Father. As we read in 2 Corinthians 5:21, "God made him who had no sin to be sin for us, so that in him we might become the righteousness of God" (NIV).

I can write these words. I can say, truly, that the Father abandoned the Son for our sake, for the salvation of the world.

But what does salvation mean in 2015? What does it mean that God would let Jesus his only son feel the pain of the cross? The pain of being lynched as a Black male in public?

Kirk Franklin once said, "The problem with gospel music today, people need to get high off something spiritual, and I'm the holy dope dealer. I got this drug, I got this Jesus rock. And you can have a type of high that you've never experienced."[5]

To be fair, Franklin probably spoke in such shocking terms to capture the attention of Vibe's youthful, hip hop-oriented readership.

Still, with his use of the term Jesus "rock" (the street name for crack cocaine),

---

4. James H. Cone, The Cross and the Lynching Tree (Maryknoll, NY: Orbis Books, 2011).
5. Obery M. Hendricks Jr., "'I Am the Holy Dope Dealer': The Problem with Gospel Music Today," in The Journal of the Interdenominational Theological Center 27, Nos. 1 and 2 (Fall 1999/Spring 2000): 12, 13.

Franklin himself characterizes his music as an opiate, a drug.

In a nutshell, that is the basic problem with a lot of the gospel we hear and the story of the cross being preached today—it's entertainment.

That kind of painless, cross-less preaching is what some theologians call "clowning."

Clowning-style singing and preaching has performance orientation, with emphasis on "wrecking the house" and shameless appeals to emotion, to the dance, and to the whoop and no real appeal to the needs of the people.

We have to preach a Gospel that must stop reducing the causes of human suffering to weak faith or poor morality on the part of the victim or to ethereal, disembodied sources for which no one has responsibility.

As with a drug, sensations and emotions have come to be its focus. Like a drug, its primary goal is not to empower its users to change reality, but simply to change the way they feel.

Like a drug, it temporarily lifts the people's despair yet, in direct contradistinction to the prophetic mandate of the spirituals, leaves the causes of that despair virtually unaddressed, unscathed, even unmentioned.

A lot of the Gospel we hear and preach doesn't attempt to free the people but simply seeks to make them feel good.

I am thankful that God—while Jesus was on the cross—shows us with the fourth word that the pain was real, the separation was real, and it hurt. I almost wish the fourth word was "I hurt!"

Because yes, church, the Gospel hurts! Yes, church, oppression hurts! Yes, Lake City, sin hurts, and any time you deal with sin, it's gonna hurt. My God, why do I hurt?

Chapter 6
The Real Question Is What Color
You Will Decide to Represent

"Unless we start to fight and defeat the enemies in our own country, poverty and racism, and make our talk of equality and opportunity ring true, we are exposed in the eyes of the world as hypocrites when we talk about making people free."—Shirley Chisholm, first Black woman to be elected to Congress (in 1968) and to run for president (in 1972)

"History has shown us that courage can be contagious, and hope can take on a life of its own."—Michelle Obama, first Black First Lady of the United States

Sermon Site Media Tag: Beyond the Veil—Color Change Christians
Contributed by Amiri Hooker, February 6, 2016
12,982 views before rejection
Scripture: Exodus 34:29-35
Denomination: United Methodist

About the sermon:

The convergence of Transfiguration Sunday and Black History Month presents a unique opportunity to celebrate both the transformative power of faith and the rich legacy of African-American contributions to history and culture. These two observances, though distinct, share common themes of change, resilience, and the pursuit of justice. Transfiguration Sunday commemorates the biblical event when Jesus, accompanied by disciples Peter, James, and John, experienced a profound transformation on the mountaintop. The transfiguration revealed Jesus's divine nature, shining with radiant glory. This event symbolizes the transformative power of faith and serves as a reminder of the hope and renewal that spiritual journeys can bring. Black History Month is a dedicated time to celebrate the achievements, struggles, and contributions of African Americans throughout history. It emerged from the desire to highlight the often-overlooked legacies of Black leaders, artists, inventors, and activists who have played pivotal roles in shaping American society.

This was one of three sermons that looked at the idea of transformation and change based on race and skin color. What does it mean to consider changing who and what God has created you to become?

Excerpt from rejection:

"The only reason for this rejection has to do with the previous submission about the Hebrew in Jeremiah 13:23. Once this is revised we will approve it again to be up on the platform. Below is the paragraph for your reference. 'But church, if you are really serious about coming into the presence of God, you need to change color. Wednesday night during Bible study, we dealt with the text Jeremiah 13:23—can a leopard change its spots or an Ethiopian change his skin?' And as we discussed the fact that the original language of the text could be read as (would) be cause to the biblical writer the idea of a leopard or an Ethiopian wanting to change made no sense.'"

Reflection:

The biblical writers' approach to race and skin color is one that emphasizes unity, love, and the shared humanity of all individuals. While racism has plagued societies for centuries, examining the biblical perspective can help us gain valuable insights into promoting inclusivity and harmony. By embracing the teachings of love, compassion, and respect for all people, regardless of their race or ethnicity, we can work toward building a more equitable and just world for everyone. The core message of the Bible is one of love, compassion, and the inherent value of every individual. Throughout the scriptures, God is depicted as a benevolent creator who loves all people equally, regardless of their background or appearance. This message of universal love can be found in verses like Galatians 3:28, which states, "There is neither Jew nor Gentile, neither slave nor free, nor is there male and female, for you are all one in Christ Jesus" (NIV). Yet for many Black- and Brown-skinned children, the text may have been more impactful if it stated: "There is neither light-skinned or dark-skinned, neither Black nor White" This is best illustrated in the practice of skin bleaching, where individuals use creams or other methods to lighten their skin color.

This is a complex and sensitive issue that has garnered attention worldwide. In many communities, particularly among people of African descent, the desire to change skin color through bleaching is a prevalent yet controversial phenomenon.

One significant factor behind the desire to bleach skin is the historical legacy of Eurocentric beauty standards. During colonization and the transatlantic slave trade, European features were idealized and considered the epitome of beauty. This deeply ingrained perception led to the marginalization of Black features and skin tones, perpetuating the belief that lighter skin is more desirable and attractive.

The history of racism in America is deeply rooted in the country's past, with slavery being one of the most significant influences on the construction of racial identities. African Americans, forcibly brought to America as slaves, were subjected to systemic oppression, discrimination, and dehumanization. Terms such as "Black" were historically used to perpetuate a narrative of inferiority and subjugation, further marginalizing the African-American community. In societies with deeply rooted colorism, individuals with lighter skin are sometimes treated with preferential treatment compared to those with darker skin. This social stigma and discrimination can contribute to a desire to lighten one's skin (i.e., change one's spots) to fit into societal beauty standards and avoid prejudice.

This is also true for mixed-race children and individuals. In certain contexts, people associate lighter skin with greater economic and social opportunities. Some may believe that lighter skin increases their chances of success in various areas of life, including education, employment, and marriage prospects.

In 2023, the issue of colorism continues to be a pressing concern within the African and African-American communities. Colorism, a form of discrimination based on skin color, has deep historical roots and has permeated societies worldwide, perpetuating harmful beliefs and attitudes about skin tones. Despite progress in the fight against racial discrimination, colorism persists as a significant challenge, impacting individuals' self-esteem, social opportunities, and overall well-being. In the modern era, media and the entertainment industry play a significant role in perpetuating colorism. Representations of beauty predominantly feature individuals with lighter skin, reinforcing the harmful idea that lighter is more desirable. In contrast, many White evangelical males would not understand these issues of race. Many young Black and Brown skinned children still sit around wishing they could change their skin color to something more akin to their White teachers and coworkers.

The Banned Sermon:
Beyond the Veil—Color Change Christians
By Amiri Hooker, February 6, 2016
Scripture: Exodus 34:29-35 (MSG)
Denomination: United Methodist

Scripture:

Exodus 34:29-35 (MSG), "When Moses came down from Mount Sinai carrying the two Tablets of The Testimony, he didn't know that the skin of his face glowed because he had been speaking with God. Aaron and all the Israelites saw Moses, saw his radiant face, and held back, afraid to get close to him. Moses called out to them. Aaron and the leaders in the community came back and Moses talked with them. Later all the Israelites came up to him and he passed on the commands, everything that God had told him on Mount Sinai. When Moses finished speaking with them, he put a veil over his face, but when he went into the presence of God to speak with him, he removed the veil until he came out. When he came out and told the Israelites what he had been commanded, they would see Moses' face, its skin glowing, and then he would again put the veil on his face until he went back in to speak with God."

Introduction:

This is a sermon that deals with the need to make real change in the way we do faith. This is also a sermon during Black History Month that covers the idea of what it means to push to be the best person in the presence of God one can possibly be.

Main body:

Did you know transformation can be a good and also be a bad thing? When we are changed or transformed what we have can be turned into what God would have. God does not deal with us on the ordinary level. When you come in contact with God, you need to come into the presence of the Almighty. You need to bring your A Game.

For decades, Black parents have told their children that in order to succeed despite racial discrimination, they need to be "twice as good"—twice as smart, twice as dependable, twice as talented. This advice can be found in everything from literature to television shows to day-to-day conversation. Now, a new paper from the National Bureau of Economic Research shows that when it comes to getting and keeping jobs, that notion might be more than just a saying.

But church, if you are really serious about coming into the presence of God, you need to change color.

Wednesday night during Bible study we dealt with the text Jeremiah 13:23, "Can a leopard change its spots, or an Ethiopian change his skin?" and we discussed the fact that the original language of the text could be read as "would," because to the biblical writer, the idea of a leopard or an Ethiopian wanting to change made no sense.

But we need to look at the idea that color is not an Old Testament concept. Folks in the Old Testament were not concerned with race but class and culture. So today I want you to know you need to change your color.

There are a lot of folks out there that are yellow. They are yellow because they are afraid to even go to God.

There are a lot of folks out there that are pink. They are soft and fear being real with what God has called them to do.

There are a lot of folks playing white, pretending to be innocent and pure and don't have a pure thought in mind.

But I tell you: It's time to change your color, because God is calling you to have a glow!

When you are close to God, you know it. When you step up to the level of God—when you make yourself ready for God, ready to approach God—yes, I am telling you it's time. Get glowing for God.

There are some keys to doing your best. One of the keys we need to teach our children during Black History Month is how is it we do our best. One of the persons that comes to mind during this month is Josephine Baker. Josephine Baker, who lived June 3, 1906, to April 12, 1975, was an American-born French dancer, singer, and actress who came to be known in various circles as the "Black Pearl," "Bronze Venus," and even the "Creole Goddess." She was the top of her profession. No one else could do what she could do or dance like she could dance, and she was sure to let the world know. She became a muse for contemporary authors, painters, designers, and sculptors, including Langston Hughes, Ernest Hemingway, F. Scott Fitzgerald, Pablo Picasso, and Christian Dior.

When I think of Moses interacting with God on the mountain, I see Moses acting in a way worthy of being in a holy place. So today I want to share with you some ways to do your best, some ways to be your best, and some ways that you can do better in America—in Black America.

Point 1: Cultivate a Good Attitude

There is scientific research that positivity attracts abundance and success. So, if you want to do your best at work, you need to cultivate and practice bringing a positive attitude with you to work.

You can create this energy by doing some very basic things such as getting a good night's sleep, especially during the work week, eating properly, and not overindulging.

You can also do that by surrounding yourself with positive people and by bringing more positive ideas into your life.

Point 2: Fuel Your Own Success

We all have a little engine inside of us that propels us along the road in our career and our life. But we have to fuel this engine, or it starts to seize up and won't move any more. We also have to lubricate the moving parts.

We do this by finding ways to introduce new ideas and concepts that we can strive to learn. That engine is sometimes called motivation, and while we can draw strength from outside to help us keep moving, ninety percent of it is about finding it inside ourselves.

Spend a little time every day to find your own fuel so that you can always do your best.

Point 3: Plan Your Own Growth

Just like motivation is an inside job so, too, is the growth of your career. Yes, it is about opportunities coming to you to take advantage of, but if you notice the people who get ahead quickly, they are standing at the door even before it opens.

So, get ready for these opportunities by developing your own growth plan at work. Think about where you want to be in five years and ten years and then put it down in writing.

Next, put your paper plan into action. Take a course, get a transfer, recruit a coach or mentor, and get to work building your own success. Always do your best by doing everything you can to make success and growth possible.

Point 4: Stop Judging Yourself

As Don Miguel Ruiz says in his book *The Fifth Agreement*, your best will differ depending on your physical and emotional state of mind.[1] You will and can certainly do better when you are well-rested versus being stressed-over. And doing your best does not mean that you overdo things or keep working all night in some desperate attempt to finally finish that overdue project.

It means that you give your work your full focus and attention while you are working on it, and then you move on to the next thing and do the same.

And when you leave that first piece, you do not judge or second-guess yourself. You acknowledge that you did your best, and you just move on.

I know this is football Sunday and the Sunday we deal with Super Bowl. But I want to look at the other American sport. One of America's most iconic and inspiring stories is when Jackie Robinson broke baseball's color line in 1947. It is difficult today to summon the excitement that greeted Robinson's achievement. The dignity with which Robinson handled his encounters with racism—including verbal and physical abuse on the field and in hotels, restaurants, trains, and elsewhere—drew public attention to the issue, stirred the consciences of many White Americans, and

---

1. Don Miguel Ruiz, Don Jose Ruiz, and Janet Mills, *The Fifth Agreement* (San Rafael, CA: Amber-Allen Publishing, 2010).

gave Black Americans a tremendous boost of pride and self-confidence.

Martin Luther King Jr. once told Dodgers star Don Newcombe, another former Negro Leaguer, "You'll never know what you and Jackie and Roy [Campanella] did to make it possible to do my job."

You see, when Moses went up into the mountain, just as when the disciples went up into the mountains with Jesus on the day of transfiguration, the key was not about staying on the mountain. It is about how you come back down and change the lives of the people. Moses, like the disciples, as King said, made the job of God easy by spreading the message. So, I tell you!

And when you go to God and you have been with God, God has given you something to work with. God has given Black America something—a new plane, a new mind, and a new body, a new message to come down. To tell and touch the people's lives this time.

Yes, it's time to glow for God, change for God, and be real for God's message.

Chapter 7
The Key to Peace is Color Blindness

"Some well-meaning folks think if we stop talking about racism, it'll magically disappear, like the smell of an errant fart. But like a fart, people might try to be polite and ignore it, but everyone knows it's there. Avoidance has never been a great tactic in solving any problem.
—*Luvvie Ajayi Jones*, I'm Judging You: The Do-Better Manual [1]

"The language of color blindness—like the language of 'not racist'—is a mask to hide racism. 'Our Constitution is color-blind,' U.S. Supreme Court Justice John Harlan proclaimed in his dissent to Plessy v. Ferguson, the case that legalized Jim Crow segregation in 1896. 'The White race deems itself to be the dominant race in this country,' Justice Harlan went on. 'I doubt not, it will continue to be for all time, if it remains true to its great heritage.' A color-blind Constitution for a White-supremacist America."—*Ibram X. Kendi*, How to Be an Antiracist [2]

Sermon Site Media Tag: Can a Black Man Change His Color?
Contributed by Amiri Hooker, February 27, 2016
10,936 views before rejection
Scripture: Jeremiah 13:21-27
Denomination: United Methodist

About the sermon:

This is another sermon that looks at the question of change and wonders at the idea of race as a variable that, if manipulated, could improve one status and life. This

---

1. Luvvie Ajayi, *I'm Judging You: The Do-Better Manual* (New York: Henry Holt, 2016).
2. Ibram X. Kendi, *How to Be an Antiracist* (London: One World, 2019).

sermon is not about the wish many have to change their skin color by skin lightening or tanning. This sermon focuses more on the idea that many in the modern area have a concept of skin color idolatry. This is a sad commentary when many core teachings of Christianity emphasize the importance of love, equality, and compassion for all humanity.

This sermon also seeks to dispel the notion of color blindness. Color blindness suggests that people should not see or acknowledge racial differences, which can be perceived as dismissing the unique experiences and challenges faced by various racial and ethnic groups, including African Americans. Instead of celebrating diversity, color blindness can inadvertently erase cultural identities and perpetuate systemic inequalities.

Excerpt from rejection:

"Unfortunately, some of the content contained in this sermon cannot be approved at this time due to the following concerns. You stated that the rhetorical question in Jeremiah 13:23 contains in it a Hiphil Imperfect. However, the first half of the verse about the color of a man's skin or the spots on a leopard only contain Qal. Hiphil's do come later in the verse but are not related to what you are describing and are in an infinitive construct. All the major translations of Scripture translate this as 'can,' making it rhetorical, rather than 'should/would,' which would not fit at all with the context of the passage. Jeremiah's point is not 'why would they change' but rather, 'they are not able to change … therefore, you who are accustomed to doing evil cannot do good.' Unfortunately, everything following in your sermon cannot be approved because it is flowing out of this misunderstanding of the Hebrew and reading the Bible through a contemporary lens rather than an exegetical-historical-theological lens.

"Later in your sermon, you also said, 'Jesus said for some people culture/race is even stronger than the Word of God (Mark 7:7-8). Consequently, people read the scriptures through their Caucasian/Western, Afro-centric, Hispanic or Asian lenses.' Jesus is talking about the teachings of traditions, not culture/race.

"Finally, you mentioned, 'It truly time we stop letting White surmises and the whiteness of Jesus prevent us from being faithful to God.' However, no faithful expositor of the Word would say that Jesus is Black or White. He is a Jew from Bethlehem."

Reflection:

Studies have shown that individuals with lighter skin may have better job prospects, higher incomes, and greater access to education and opportunities compared to their darker-skinned counterparts.[3] This disparity perpetuates systemic inequality and reinforces the correlation between lighter skin and success. Colorism can lead to internalized racism, where individuals with darker skin may internalize negative stereotypes and develop lower self-esteem.

On the other hand, colorism can also lead to idolatry of race. White supremacy, a belief system that promotes the superiority of White individuals over other racial groups, stands in stark contrast to the principles of equality, love, and justice that Christianity upholds. White supremacy, rooted in the idolatry of race, contradicts these fundamental values, promoting division and discrimination based on skin color. Idolatry of race, or the worship of one's racial identity to the detriment of others, fuels division and hatred counter to the values that God would support. White supremacy seeks to elevate one group at the expense of others, contrary to God's call for unity and inclusivity. White supremacy, as a manifestation of idolatry of race, reinforces oppressive systems that marginalize and discriminate against people of color.

However, people of color need also to be careful not to see their skin color as a free pass to grace. People of color can also fall into the trap of idolizing their race or the race of others. Idolatry of race perpetuates the dehumanization of individuals from marginalized racial groups, undermining the inherent worth and dignity of all human beings. Such views contradict the divine principle of seeing the sacredness in every person. As spiritual beings, it is essential to recognize the intrinsic worth and dignity of every individual, irrespective of their racial background.

The Bible teaches that God created all human beings in his image (Genesis 1:27). Our physical appearances, including our skin tones, are part of God's divine design. Changing one's skin color would be an attempt to alter a fundamental aspect of God's creation, which goes against his intended purpose. God's creation is a testament to the beauty and diversity of humanity. People come in a multitude of skin tones, each reflecting the richness of cultural heritage and history. While some individuals may contemplate changing their skin color, it is essential to recognize that God intentionally created this diversity. Each skin color reflects the cultural heritage and history of various communities. As children of God, we are called to love and accept ourselves and others just as God created us. Changing one's skin color negates the inherent beauty of God's creation and perpetuates harmful societal beauty standards. Let us embrace our unique identities and love ourselves and one another.

Jesus addresses the issue of placing cultural traditions or race above the Word of God in Mark 7:7-8. While the specific context of this passage is related to religious traditions, it can also be applied to the broader concept of cultural prejudices, in-

---

3. Kristen R. Moore, David R. Williams, and Donna D. Baird, "Disparities by Skin Color among Young African-American Women," *Journal of Racial and Ethnic Health Disparities* 8, no. 4 (September 4, 2020): 1002–11, https://doi.org/10.1007/s40615-020-00856-x.

cluding those based on race. In this passage, Jesus criticizes the Pharisees and scribes for elevating their man-made traditions over the commandments of God. He quotes Isaiah 29:13, saying, "'These people honor me with their lips, but their hearts are far from me. They worship me in vain; their teachings are merely human rules'" (Matthew 15:8-9 NIV). Race-based prejudices can be understood as an extension of cultural biases. When cultural or racial identities are held with undue supremacy, it can lead to the exclusion or discrimination of others based on their cultural or racial background.

While the specific context of Mark 7:7-8 is related to religious traditions, Jesus's message challenges us to examine our attitudes toward cultural and racial biases as well. Placing culture or race above the principles of love and inclusion undermines the teachings of Jesus, who called us to love one another unconditionally. As followers of Christ, it is our duty to break down barriers, challenge prejudices, and embrace the diverse creation of God.

By doing so, we can work toward a world where cultural and racial unity prevails and the love of God shines brightly among all people, regardless of their cultural or racial background.

The Banned Sermon:
Can a Black Man Change His Color?
Contributed by Amiri Hooker, February 27, 2016
Scripture: Jeremiah 13:21-27
Denomination: United Methodist

Scripture text:

Jeremiah 13:23 (MSG), "Can an African change skin? Can a leopard get rid of its spots? So what are the odds on you doing good, you who are so long-practiced in evil?"

Introduction:

This is a Black history sermon based on the idea of idolatry and race. The prophet Jeremiah, in no uncertain terms, goes on to declare to Judah, the ancient people of God, that just as there is no desire on the part of either the eye-catching leopard or the black-skinned African to change their spots; thus Judah should have no desire to change their God.

Main body:

Jerusalem had no power to protect the people in its country. It was like a shepherd who could not look after his sheep. The enemy from the north was Babylon, who was attacking Judah already. Judah had tried to make Babylon a political friend. But Babylon would rule Judah.

The people did not believe that such trouble would happen to them. They wanted to know why it would happen. They were like many people who ask this: "Why should that happen to me?"

Jeremiah said that it was because of Judah's great sins. What was this great sin? Running after, chasing after other gods. For some reason during the time of Jeremiah, the people had a hard time being faithful to God, and when you prostitute and cheat on God, nothing good comes after it.

Today we celebrate the last Sunday in Black History Month, what many call Black Pride Sunday. And in a year following the Black Lives Matter summer and a weekend following the epic fight for the Black vote in South Carolina between Bernie Sanders and Hillary Clinton, one would ask the eternal question: Why do Black folks have it so hard?

Why is it that Black America is having it so hard?

Well, one example might be found in the message of Jeremiah. The prophet was clear that the punishment was coming because of the sin of idolatry. The greatest sin in the Bible by far is the sin of idolatry. Idolatry is the main reason why God rebuked and judged the nation of Israel. (Read the major and minor prophets as well as the books of Kings and Chronicles.) Idolatry is when we violate the first of the Ten Commandments, which says, "You shall have no other gods before me" (Exodus 20:3 NIV). It is when we put something or someone first in our life before the living and true God. Idolatry is the root cause of all other sins—which is why the first two commandments dealt with this.

So, we see in the text that the Lord's punishment would be like the enemy who tears off their clothes. They would appear naked. That happened to prostitutes to make them ashamed in public. It's like putting all their business in the street. During this time in the Bible, putting your dirty laundry in the street was the worst thing that could be done. Hosea spoke about his wife in that way (Hosea 2:3, 10).

And then we come to the part of the text I find great. In verse 23, the Bible seems to be making the point that it seemed impossible for the nation to change its wicked behavior.

It is impossible for a Black man to change the color of his skin.

A leopard is a large animal like a lion. It has small black spots all over its fur. It cannot remove its spots.

Judah had not obeyed the Lord's laws for a long time. Judah's bad behavior had become a habit.

Many of us have misread the text as "can." I am so glad I can read the text in its original Hebrew and don't depend on Peterson or James. Because a careful reading of the Hebrew in which the prophet Jeremiah initially wrote would indicate that the Hebrew word, *yakal*, which is to be correctly translated as "can," is not in the text at all. Instead, what we find at the onset of the rhetorical question is (in technical Hebrew grammar) a Hiphil Imperfect, which can best be translated as "would."

Thus, the question that is really in the text is suggestive. That is, the rhetorical question should really be translated as: "Would a leopard change its spots or an Ethiopian change his skin?"

And as a rhetorical question, the implied response would then be: "Of course not! Why would either the leopard or the Ethiopian want to change its or his appearance?"

Now what this shows us is how important translations of just a word or two can make in reading the Bible—the difference in "can" and "would." If someone asked Black America, "Can you change your skin color?" that is an entirely different question than "Would you?" But I'm asking you today, church: Would you change your skin color? With all the oppression and hate and suffering we have been though, would you like to take a pill or a shot and change your race?

I still hope for the most of us the answer is "no." But there might be some in the number who would say, "Yeah, why not change my color?"

And that's because you don't have a clue why we are suffering.

We who want to trust in the Lord and stay the color the Lord made us are clear that future punishment comes from the Lord. It comes because the people trust false gods.

The Lord hated the false religion that happened in the hills and in the fields. The Babylonians would attack Jerusalem. Jeremiah thought about what would happen. He was very sad when he thought about that. His question, "How long?" showed Jeremiah's slight hope that Judah might change. Perhaps Judah would become the Lord's loyal nation. Jeremiah knew the Lord's punishment was certain. But his great wish was that his people would return to the Lord. The Lord had chosen Judah to serve him.

The following are three signs of idolatry in the church based on my perspective of serving as a lead pastor for twenty-five years:

One, the idol of worship/entertainment: There are many believers who flock to churches that have skilled singers and music primarily to get entertained. Consequently, many of the believers don't realize they are putting self-gratification and entertainment before true worship. Years ago, many churches would not even have musical instruments and people would flock to churches anyway—even though the congregation only used hymnals and sang a cappella for worship.

But now, it is very common for pastors to budget a large amount of money

Chapter 8
The Powerful Need to Remember to Forgive

"The very serious function of racism … is distraction. It keeps you from doing your work. It keeps you explaining, over and over again, your reason for being. Somebody says you have no language and so you spend twenty years proving that you do. Somebody says your head isn't shaped properly so you have scientists working on the fact that it is. Somebody says that you have no art so you dredge that up. Somebody says that you have no kingdoms and so you dredge that up. None of that is necessary."—Toni Morrison speech, "A Humanist View" [1]

"I learned that racism, like most systems of oppression, isn't about bad people doing terrible things to people who are different from them but instead is a way of maintaining power for certain groups at the expense of others."
—Alicia Garza, The Purpose of Power: How We Come Together When We Fall Apart [2]

Sermon Site Media Tag:#MyBlackHistory, An African Context for an African Faith
Contributed by Amiri Hooker, February 11, 2022
76 views before rejection
Scripture: Genesis 45:3-11
Denomination: United Methodist

About the sermon:
This sermon is based on the idea that what happens in Africa does not stay in

1. Toni Morrison, "A Humanist View," Transcript of speech given at Portland State University Library, May 30, 1975, https://www.mackenzian.com/wp-content/uploads/2014/07/Transcript_PortlandState_TMorrison.pdf.
2. Alicia Garza, *The Purpose of Power: How We Come Together When We Fall Apart* (London: One World, 2020).

Africa but has helped to shape the experiment we call America. The sermon looks at the story of Joseph, son of Jacob and Rachel, and how he was betrayed by his brothers, sold into slavery, and later imprisoned. Joseph faced immense adversity throughout his life. In the Black American experience, this narrative of struggle and survival holds significant resonance. Like Joseph, enslaved Africans were forcibly taken from their homeland, separated from their families, and subjected to unimaginable suffering and cruelty. The concept of freedom and liberation is another parallel shared between Joseph and Black Americans. Joseph's eventual rise to power in Egypt allowed him to liberate his people from famine and hardship. His position of authority enabled him to look into the concepts of forgiveness in the lives of his family and community.

In this sermon, we use Joseph's themes of divine providence and perseverance to resonate deeply within the church community, providing them with a source of inspiration and comfort. The story of Joseph is a timeless tale of forgiveness, resilience, and redemption. Joseph's journey inspires us to let go of bitterness and seek reconciliation, and the sermon hopes to link this concept of forgiveness and reconciliation to be a vital part of Black History Month.

Excerpt from rejection:

"Although it is great progress to have a Black History Month where everyone can learn about the contributions of Black Americans, it is also so very limiting. You can't celebrate Black history if you don't go beyond the 'look at what I made' and deal with the 'look who made me.'"

Reflection:

The narrative of Black church history/Black history is not confined solely to the shackles of slavery but rather traces its profound roots to a time before the transatlantic journey began. To understand the vibrant tapestry of the Black church, we must delve into the centuries-old history that predates the dark days of bondage. Egypt's history spans millennia, boasting one of the world's oldest and most influential civilizations. From the Great Pyramids of Giza to the captivating hieroglyphics and cultural achievements, Egypt's contributions have left an indelible mark on human history. The ancient Egyptians were a diverse people, and some scholars maintain that they were of African descent. Egypt holds a prominent place in the biblical narrative, featuring in the stories of the Hebrew patriarchs and the Exodus account. The Bible tells of Joseph's sojourn in Egypt as a slave, his rise to power, and how God used him to preserve life during a great famine.

Furthermore, the Exodus, led by Moses, is a pivotal event that embodies the theme of liberation from oppression and God's faithfulness to his people. This narrative of resilience and freedom resonates deeply with the African-American experience, making Egypt a place of shared history.

In addition to its biblical significance, Egypt is home to one of the oldest Christian communities in the world: the Coptic Christians. The Coptic Church traces its roots back to the apostolic era and has preserved ancient Christian traditions and liturgy. Understanding the historical impact of the Coptic Christian legacy can strengthen the connection between Black history and Christianity, fostering a sense of shared faith and heritage. As we embark on the journey of celebrating Black history, Egypt stands as a compelling starting point. By recognizing Egypt's importance in the tapestry of Black history, we embrace a more comprehensive and inclusive understanding of our shared past.

The truth is that the church needs to be forgiven, for like the brothers of Joseph, they have come to this time of church transition and totally forgotten their own history.

The Reverend Albert Cleage Jr. articulated a transformative, textured, multivalent, and revolutionary theology through his sermonic militancy. There was a common sentiment among Black revolutionaries, militants, and agnostic contributors to the Black Power movement that Christianity was "the White man's religion" and offered no productive or prophetic path forward.[3] Conversely, in his sermon "An Epistle to Stokely," Cleage offered a response to that. Using rhetorical strategies of disruption, rhetorical hermeneutics, reconstitutive rhetoric, parrhesia, and nomos, Cleage pointed out that often it is better to embrace (and ordain) Black revolutionaries for their own political protection and for the church's social-political advancement.

The church can only advance the goal of celebrating Black history by spending equal time in recovering the proper context for biblical faith as an African Old Testament story. In 1968, James Baldwin gave an address to the World Council of Churches during which he said: "The most serious thing that has happened in the world today and in the Christian conscience is that Christians, having rationalized their crimes for so long, though they live with them every day and see evidence of them every day, put themselves out of touch with themselves."[4]

He discerned that the real issue was not just the crimes White people committed against Black people but also their denial of those crimes—a denial that springs from the internal conflict they experience when they realize their choices are at odds with their values.

In an essay titled "The White Problem," Baldwin explains, "I'm not talking about the crime; I'm talking about denying what one does. This is a much more sinister

3. Earle J. Fisher, *The Reverend Albert Cleage Jr. and the Black Prophetic Tradition: A Reintroduction of the Black Messiah* (New York: Lexington Books, 2021).

4. James Baldwin, *The Price of the Ticket: Collected Nonfiction 1948-1985* (Boston: Beacon Press, 2021).

matter." [5]

Slavery was White America's original sin, but denial of this crime has led White people to invent justifications that have produced racial prejudice. This denial and justification, then, (rather than the original crime of slavery) is Baldwin's primary focus. Thus, forgiveness has to start with the guilty party acknowledging their crime. Throughout his life, Baldwin called for a reckoning with the sins of poor biblical scholarship about race. He believed that a genuine confrontation with this issue was necessary for societal healing and reconciliation. The time has come to call on people of faith to reexamine their understanding of the scriptures, confront their biases, and actively work toward dismantling the systems of oppression perpetuated by poor biblical interpretations.

In the wake of the tragic Charleston church massacre on June 17, 2015, the world watched in shock and grief as nine innocent lives were taken by a heinous act of violence. However, amid the darkness, a remarkable and inspiring act of forgiveness emerged from the hearts of the victims' families. In the face of unspeakable loss, they demonstrated the transformative power of forgiveness, sparking a global conversation on reconciliation and the ramifications of this profound act of grace. The victims' families' act of forgiveness sent a powerful message of healing and unity to their community and the world. They demonstrated the radical power of love and grace, highlighting that forgiveness is not about condoning the act but releasing the burden of anger and hatred that can consume one's soul. Their act of forgiveness became a rallying cry for racial reconciliation and social justice, inspiring others to seek common ground amid division.

All sermons that seek a truthful history should also do the same thing.

The Banned Sermon:
#MyBlackHistory, An African Context for an African Faith
By Amiri Hooker, February 11, 2022
Scripture: Genesis 45:3-11
Denomination: United Methodist

Scripture text:

Genesis 45:7-8, 15, "But God sent me ahead of you to preserve for you a remnant on earth and to save your lives by a great deliverance. So then, it was not you who sent me here, but God. He made me father to Pharaoh, lord of his entire household and ruler of all Egypt. … And he kissed all his brothers and wept over them. After-

---

5. James Baldwin, "The White Problem," in *The Cross of Redemption: Uncollected Writings*, ed. Randall Kenan (New York: Vintage, 2011).

ward his brothers talked with him."
Introduction:

To get a good sense of who Joseph, the father of the pharaoh, was we can compare him with the great Black historic figure Nelson Mandela, who also showed great compassion and forgiveness.

Main body:

The narrative of Black people, as taught by most American schools, begins with slavery. But that's not where our story begins; our story begins in Africa. For each Black American, our story begins in a certain part of Africa, with an ethnic history, culture, and community that is thriving. Scholars such as Cain Hope Felder, Cheikh Anta Diop, Walter McCray, and others have spent enormous time and intellectual energies, some making it their life's work, proving that the people of the Bible were not White. The aforementioned scholars have more than adequately challenged and refuted the notion that White people comprised the biblical community. Therefore, this work does not belabor their well-made conclusions but advances the notion that the people of the Bible were mainly northern Africans and, therefore, Black people.

In that the biblical story begins in Africa, this makes the biblical Hebrews immediate descendants of Africans. Also, the number of times that Ethiopia, Egypt, and Israel are mentioned in the Bible suggests that the African landmass is referenced more than any other geographical region in biblical times, making it the focus of the biblical story. Thus, I feel to get a good sense of who Joseph, the father of the Pharaoh, was we can compare him with a great historic figure who also showed great compassion and forgiveness.

I was introduced to Nelson Mandela through a story we studied in the Children's Defense Fund. I vividly remember sharing about Mandela—that he was detained on Robben Island by the apartheid government and that no one knew how he looked.

Unresolved anger leads to bitterness, hostility, mistrust, and, in most cases, revenge. Believe me, Nelson Mandela being kept in prison for twenty-seven years should have brought enough bitterness, hostility, mistrust, and revenge on him. But the day he put his foot outside of prison, he spoke forgiveness.

Similar to Joseph in Genesis 45, the years Joseph spent in slavery and prison brought enough bitterness on him to not forgive his brothers for what they had done to him. Even worse was the anger that Joseph did not display against God for allowing this to happen to him.

Read Genesis 45:1-15. Joseph had enough reason to be angry at his brothers; the story of Joseph is filled with pain, deceit, jealousy, and also lies. In Genesis 45:1-28 we learn how Joseph responded to those lies—not through revenge but rather through reconciliation.

I remember the day when Nelson Mandela was released from prison. The whole world gathered around TVs and along the road. For the non-Whites in South Africa, it was a joyous occasion, but for White people it was also a time of fear and uncertainty.

I remember hearing on national TV and newspaper reports about White people's fear and how they were stocking up food and preparing for war, unsure of what might come in the future.

I also remember Nelson Mandela`s first public speech, which he made on the day of his release. It is similar to that of Joseph in Genesis 45:4: "I am your brother Joseph, the one you sold into Egypt."

"Friends, comrades, and fellow South-Africans. I greet you all in the name of peace, democracy, and freedom for all!" Mandela said.[6]

In Chapter 45 there is a genuine yearning for reconciliation—a Joseph reaching out to his brothers, a Nelson Mandela reaching out to his brothers and sisters, Black and White, rich and poor, sharing forgiveness. For Joseph, reconciliation was achieved through his sincerity and forgiveness of his brothers for the evil they have done to him. For Nelson Mandela, his first public words were forgiveness against the evil of apartheid.

Point 1: Forgiveness is a vital part of the Christian experience.

Forgiveness is necessary in terms of our relationship with God and also our fellow brothers and sisters. In Mathew 6:14-15 we're told, "For if you forgive other people when they sin against you, your heavenly Father will also forgive you. But if you do not forgive others their sins, your Father will not forgive your sins" (NIV).

Forgiveness is an essential part of our responsibility toward others, both friends and enemies.

Forgiveness is also a part of Black history. The Black church and its leadership has to take seriously the ethics of Jesus that we are to forgive.

The lesson of forgiveness in this passage is particularly poignant; combined with Joseph's rags-to-riches story, it is something like a fairy tale.

Unfortunately, those lessons are entwined with a deeply problematic theological gloss: that the human trafficking in the story was a tool of God to save the lives of Joseph and his family from the impending famine (v. 5-8), justifying the actions of his brothers in selling him into slavery.

Point 2: Joseph experienced slavery.

While that narrative device makes for great theater in the story of Joseph, it paints

---

6. Nelson Mandela, *Long Walk to Freedom: The Autobiography of Nelson Mandela* (Boston: Little, Brown, 1994).

an unrealistic glaze over the institution of slavery in and beyond the Bible.

Joseph's experience of slavery in the narrative was one in a million and does not mitigate against the unjust dehumanizing institution utilized by the Egyptians and other ancient peoples, including the Israelites, or American chattel slavery in North and South America and the Caribbean, or the contemporary sexual trafficking of women, girls, and boys.

The claim of verse 8—"it was not you who sent me here but God"—should perhaps be understood in this story as Joseph's perception of his circumstances and not as a broader religious sanction of slavery, human trafficking, or any other social ill over which an individual triumphs.

Joseph does what so many people do, which is he tries to make sense out of what he has experienced by drawing on his own limited understanding of God.

The focus on Joseph, his perceptions and his experiences in the narrative is a reminder that biblical literature, like all literature, has its own perspectives and biases.

The text is not interested in the well-being of any of Pharaoh's other slaves and indeed has reported on Pharaoh's idiosyncratic practices of imprisoning, freeing, and executing them at will in Genesis 40:20-22.

Today's lesson presents an opportunity to think about the claim that the God of the scriptures is the God of all and the Israelite perspective in the scriptures that God is on their side and not that of the Egyptians or the Canaanites or any other peoples.

While subsequent biblical writings will proclaim a God of universal fidelity and justice, this is not one of them.

Black history students and church readers have been quick historically to identify ourselves with the Israelites. As a result, many have never thought about the fate of the ordinary Egyptian, Canaanite, Babylonian, Persian, and other peoples who are decimated at the margins of the Israelite scriptures.

Point 3: Joseph himself stands as a bridge between cultures.

Joseph lives as an Egyptian with an Egyptian name, Zaphenath-Paneah, and an Egyptian wife, Asenath, (see Genesis 41:45). Their children Ephraim and Manasseh (and the tribes they represent) are half-Egyptian.

His brothers Judah and Simeon also marry and have children with women from the surrounding communities (see Genesis 38 and 46:10). His grandfather Laban, Rachel's father (who was also his great uncle as the brother of his grandmother Rebekah), was an Aramean (Genesis 25:20).

And his great-grandparents Abraham and Sarah were from Chaldea, which would later become Babylonia and, in our time, Iraq.

Joseph's complicated family history teaches us that Israelite identity was a cultural and religious one and not an ethnic or even national one in his time—and for some time to come.

You need to understand that in Joseph's story the Israelites and Egyptians are not pitted against one another. There will be enough food for all because of his stewardship. Indeed, the later oppressive relationship between the Egyptians and the Israelites will develop because of the ascension of a Pharaoh who does not remember Joseph, who does not know anything about him or what he did for both of their peoples (Exodus 1:8).

Point 4: We are called to remember Joseph.

Remembering Joseph, telling his story, means remembering that some family relationships are deeply troubled, even violent.

Remembering Joseph means reminding ourselves that, even in the most deeply troubled family that has experienced unimaginable rupture, forgiveness and healing are possible.

Remembering Joseph and telling his story through this lesson provides an opportunity to reflect on our stewardship, generosity, and relationships with others, both neighbors and strangers.

And lastly, today's lesson with its focus on Joseph reminds us that our actions have consequences that we may not be able to foresee.

Chapter 9
We Need to Move Forward Together, Not One Step Back

"A democracy cannot thrive where power remains unchecked, and justice is reserved for a select few. Ignoring these cries and failing to respond to this movement is simply not an option—for peace cannot exist where justice is not served."—Rep. John Lewis on the George Floyd Justice in Policing Act [1]

"Press forward at all times, climbing forward toward that higher ground of the harmonious society that shapes the laws of man to the laws of God."
—Adam Clayton Powell Jr.

Sermon Site Media Tag: Don't Turn Back—Living the Spirit Life
Contributed by Amiri Hooker, June 26, 2022
255 views before rejection
Scripture: 1 Kings 19:15-21
Denomination: United Methodist

About the sermon:

This sermon was never about the courts or reproductive health. Addressing court decisions in sermons brings a sense of relevance to the issues that affect society. By connecting biblical teachings with contemporary legal rulings, religious leaders can demonstrate the timeless relevance of faith in navigating the challenges of the modern world. The focus of the sermon was about leadership and how leadership needs

---

1. Rep. John Lewis, speaking on the George Floyd Justice in Policing Act, H.R. 7120, 116th Congress, *Congressional Record*, June 25, 2020.

to transition in such a way that the second generation of leaders does not reverse the accomplishments of the first generation of leadership.

This sermon also had at its core an attempt to explore the truth behind the need for non-bivocational clergy and highlighted the importance of adapting to changing times. With more time dedicated to the church, non-bivocational clergy can focus on strategic planning, outreach, and community engagement, leading to potential growth and impact. It was also a hope of this sermon to look at the real cost to the economy of removing economic leadership to fulfill the need for pastoral.

Lastly, the sermon was a way of showing how the concept of God's creation extends beyond religious boundaries. It encompasses the intricate tapestry of life that exists in every form on our planet and beyond. One of the most profound implications of the powerful view of leadership is acknowledging the goal of furthering God's creation is its power to bridge divides.

Excerpt of rejection:

"Unfortunately, some of the content contained in this sermon cannot be approved at this time due to the following concerns. … You voiced concerns about White supremacy and the pro-life movement. Interestingly, a White woman named Margaret Sanger started Planned Parenthood. She said in 1939, 'We do not want word to go out that we want to exterminate the Negro population. …' Today, Planned Parenthood targets Black communities. 'For example, 79 percent of Planned Parenthood's surgical abortion facilities are located within walking distance of Black or Hispanic communities. The CDC and PAV report revealed that between 2007 and 2010, nearly 36 percent of all abortions in the U.S. were performed on Black children, even though Black Americans make up only 13 percent of our population. A further 21 percent of abortions were performed on Hispanics, and 7 percent more on other minority groups, for a total of 64 percent of U.S. abortions tragically performed on minority groups. Margaret Sanger would have been proud of the effects of her legacy.'[2] The ending of the constitutional right to abort a human being from the womb will save millions of lives, especially those of Blacks and other minorities. …

"We will not allow the slaughtering of human beings made in the image of God to be promoted."

Reflection:

In a world marked by social injustices, inequalities, and moral crises, the role of the community prophet and biblical spokesperson has never been more critical. These individuals serve as advocates for truth, justice, and compassion, channel-

2. Arina Grossu, "GROSSU: Margaret Sanger, Racist Eugenicist Extraordinaire," *The Washington Times*, May 5, 2014.

ing the timeless wisdom of the scriptures to address the pressing issues of our time. Community prophets and biblical spokespersons are charged with championing the social justice gospel. As a biblical spokesperson, preachers who have a responsibility to speak about history with an intention to incorporate Black history must emphasizes that the scriptures are not meant to be isolated within the confines of a sanctuary but rather to guide and inform action in the public sphere.

The topic of abortion is undeniably one of the most contentious and emotionally charged issues in modern society. For Black people, engaging in the abortion debate is far from simple, as it intersects with a myriad of historical, social, and ethical complexities. To fully understand the complexity of the abortion debate for Black people, one must recognize its historical context.

The legacy of reproductive injustice, including forced sterilizations and eugenics practices targeting Black communities, cannot be overlooked. Reproductive rights discussions must also acknowledge the socioeconomic disparities faced by many Black individuals and families. Limited access to quality health care and contraceptive resources, combined with systemic barriers, further complicate the abortion debate for Black communities. Some may perceive abortion as conflicting with deeply held cultural, religious, or spiritual beliefs, leading to complex internal struggles and moral considerations.

While critics may try to link Margaret Sanger to the historic reproductive injustices experienced by African Americans, it is crucial to remember that the roots of these issues run deeper than the founding of Planned Parenthood. Forced sterilizations, discriminatory policies, and the denial of reproductive autonomy have plagued African-American communities for generations. These injustices are systemic and not solely attributable to any single individual. Arguments about Sanger's supposed intentions have little substantial impact on African-American understanding of reproductive rights. Instead, African-American perspectives on reproductive rights are shaped by a rich and diverse history of advocacy, led by influential figures within the community.

The United States Supreme Court has historically played a crucial role in shaping the nation's laws and upholding fundamental rights. For the African-American community, landmark decisions by the court have been pivotal in advancing civil rights and justice. However, recent trends in the court's decisions have sparked concerns over the potential damage to race relations and justice. The current Supreme Court's decisions have far-reaching implications for future cases involving race relations and justice. As bedrock precedents are overturned or weakened, it sets a precedent for future rulings, potentially further eroding hard-won protections for the African-American community. The pursuit of justice and equality has been the driving force behind the United States Supreme Court's landmark decisions throughout history.

Thurgood Marshall's illustrious career was marked by tireless advocacy for civil rights and social justice. As the chief counsel for the NAACP Legal Defense and Educational Fund, Marshall led the legal team in landmark cases such as Brown v. Board of Education, which desegregated public schools. His unwavering commitment to equality laid the groundwork for future advancements in civil rights, including reproductive rights. Marshall firmly believed in the principle of reproductive autonomy as a fundamental right protected by the Constitution. He recognized that personal decisions regarding reproduction were deeply intimate and private matters, and the government should not infringe upon individual choices regarding family planning. That is the question of who controls the body and birth, not which political party is paying for the paper the decisions are written on.

The importance of the Supreme Court's decisions on reproductive rights cannot be understated, as they directly impact the fundamental freedoms and choices of millions of Americans.

The Banned Sermon:
Don't Turn Back—Living the Spirit Life
Contributed by Amiri Hooker, June 26, 2022
Scripture: 1 Kings 19:15-21
Denomination: United Methodist

Scripture text:
1 Kings 19:21 (NIV), "So Elisha left him and went back. He took his yoke of oxen and slaughtered them. He burned the plowing equipment to cook the meat and gave it to the people, and they ate. Then he set out to follow Elijah and became his servant."

Introduction:
The Supreme Court opinion on *Roe v. Wade* is going backward. The Bible is absolutely pro-abundant life, but not in a pro-life political way. It's a theological perspective of life beginning with birth, not conception.

Main body:
The call of Elisha is not like other prophetic call narratives in the Old Testament. The first stage of Elisha's new call is to be a follower and servant—a disciple, as it were—of this prophet of change. Elisha will later be described as the man "who used to pour water on the hands of Elijah" (2 Kings 3:11). The Lord tells Elijah to anoint Elisha as a prophet in his place (1 Kings 19:16), language usually reserved for kings

or priests, and such an apprenticeship with the prophet likely implied succession.

Elisha's call narrative rightly makes one think of vocation and discipleship. How do we recognize God's call in our lives? What signs of our talents and gifts have we seen in the past, and what must we give up in embracing the future God is making for us? How have we seen God's work manifested in mentors, friends, or strangers? Have we apprenticed ourselves to scarcity and fear or to abundance and hope?

There is, however, something that caught my attention studying this text this week. In the text, Elijah went straight out and found Elisha, son of Shaphat, in a field where there were twelve pairs of yoked oxen at work plowing. Elisha was in charge of the twelfth pair.

I don't want you to read over this too quickly—he was over twelve pairs of oxen! Elisha had it going on, and yet Elijah went up to him and threw his cloak over him. I mean, let's do the math. Twelve sets of tractors—that's 24 tractors. A tractor would run you about eighty thousand dollars. That's two million dollars in infrastructure, and each tractor could work forty acres a day, yielding a $700,000 annual profit. And Elisha walked away from that business to follow!

The moment of Elisha's "anointing" happens not with a pouring of oil, but rather with the throwing of Elijah's cloak, a recognized symbol of apprenticeship and a common custom among prophets. Elisha seems to understand the significance of the move.

Moreover, Elijah's mantle will continue to provide a powerful symbol of prophetic vocation and prophetic succession throughout the Elijah-Elisha narratives. When Elijah is later taken up to heaven in a chariot of fire (2 Kings 2:1-14), Elisha picks up Elijah's fallen mantle, invokes the name of the Lord, and is able to perform the same miracle with the mantle that Elijah had previously.

Thus, Elijah's draping of his mantle over Elisha foreshadows the exchange of the mantle yet to come. Though Elisha will not perform any prophetic miracles before Elijah is taken up to heaven, his actions with the oxen show that he is indeed more than a servant. He is a prophet in training.

Now watch this. When Elisha is commissioned, as a provisional elder he must quit his other profession. In other words, what Elisha had been doing must stop. He had to change his life. He had to quit his job, leave his company, and become a student of the craft of ministry.

I know the word of the day is bivocational minister, and I know a lot of preachers that have other jobs and do ministry on the side and do OK. But if you are going to be a prophet to lead the school of prophets, ministry has to be full time.

I know such-and-such pastor works at Walmart or Piggly Wiggly and they pastor just fine. But when I'm out here in these streets fighting for justice, and in school board meetings and state party meetings, a lot of these so-called pastors are at their "real job."

I know some district superintendent probably told you that to save money your church could get a part-time or local pastor. However, if you want community transformation, you need a preacher who is willing to slaughter some old oxen.

Elisha deserted the oxen, ran after Elijah, and said, "Please! Let me kiss my father and mother goodbye." Then Elisha slaughtered the oxen that had previously provided his livelihood. By doing this he made a powerful statement of vocational commitment.

There is no going back to his former way of life.

Elisha asks a question and moves forward: Let me kiss my father and mother goodbye—then I'll follow you.

"Go ahead," said Elijah, "but, mind you, don't forget what I've just done to you."

Three points and you all can be on your way.

Point 1: When you have committed to the right thing, you don't go back.

The hand of racism and White supremacy does not care how it abuses and misuses people. The idea that the pro-life movement is about pro-life is a lie, and the truth is not in it. If the pro-life movement really cared about Black and Brown babies, they would have expanded Medicare, they would have approved health care for all, and they would have fully funded Early Head Start. If the pro-life movement and the Southern Baptist Church really cared about the gospel and Jesus, they would talk about abundant life and not pro-life. Because my Bible tells of a Jesus who talked about a life of health, wealth, living wages, food to eat, peace of mind, and brotherly and sisterly love.

Hear me now, Supreme Court and legislations—I have no wish to kill babies, but this is not a question of killing. We saw that during COVID-19 when a million people in this country died. This fight around abortion is about deciding who gets have to power over life and death, who gets to control a women's body, because until birth a fetus is a part of a women's body and not a separate being.

This current fight is more a battle to say that the mother must follow the rule of men and society. The courts had it right with abortion rights and the *Roe v. Wade* decision. To go back now is not about saving a life. If you understand that in the politicized term, it's fraught with problematic racial views and exceptions and blind spots.

While many conservative White evangelicals rejoiced after the reversal of *Roe*, the reception in Black churches has often been more complicated.

As Black churches, we can't help viewing the debate through a racial lens: Black women are more likely to have abortions, according to Kaiser Family Foundation data, while government reports show they are also three times as likely as White women to die of pregnancy complications.

Reversing *Roe v. Wade* is a hollow victory if it isn't paired with more resources for young mothers to address the financial and health risks faced by Black women.

People of means are still going to find a way to get rid of an unwanted pregnancy. And for those people in impoverished communities and communities of color, if they're desperate enough, they're still going to find a way to get rid of an unwanted pregnancy. The truth is that desperation will lead Black women to seek unsafe abortions.

The real question is if Black and Brown children are not born into poverty, then who will fill the jail cells and the prison camps and work the slave-wage jobs in this country?

Point 2: To anoint is to bring life.

One of the things that is so powerful about the story of Elijah is we get to see into his pain. Though Elisha may not know anything about Elijah's dark night of the soul in the earlier part of this chapter (1 Kings 19:4), we readers have been given a glimpse of the prophet's gloom. We know that the prophetic call can be full of danger, loneliness, and despair. The prophet stands against the most powerful men in the land—the kings—and opposes their status quo.

We know that Elijah was at the point of giving up. And God's response was, "Anoint your way out of your depression." Elijah had just had a major victory against the false prophets of Baal, Israel had repented of their sins, and God had used him to stop the drought. This was a great victory. However, after great victories, we're very prone to great emotional lows.

When Elijah anointed Elisha, Elisha was not simply going to be his future replacement; he was going to be Elijah's assistant (1 Kings 19:21).

He was going to help Elijah bear the burden of ministry. In addition, Elisha would refresh Elijah.

You see when your ministry is one of anointing, it makes the situation better. I think all parts of the government, from the executive to the judicial to the legislative, could learn something from Elijah. When you are nation-building and making disciples of Jesus, the folks you select need to be about bettering life, refreshing and fulfilling hope, not politics of destruction, distortion, and distraction.

oint 3: You can't afford to go back.

After hearing God speak in a whisper and being challenged and recommissioned by him, Elijah got back to work. He left Mount Horeb, found Elisha, and anointed him, calling him to serve as his assistant and apprentice.

Likewise, one of the difficulties of battling sin is that it makes us self-centered. We become consumed with ourselves, our bad circumstances, and our future, and we tend to forget God and others. Often the best thing we can do when sin, racism, and hate are overcoming us is to getting busy focusing on and serving others.

By taking on Elisha, Elijah was going to spend a great amount of time investing in his young apprentice, somebody who would continue Elijah's work after he was gone.

Similarly, when in the battle for soul salvation, we should focus on serving our family members who need our care and attention, as well as our church members, coworkers, and especially those less fortunate than us.

No doubt, by calling Elijah to serve others, God was bringing light into the darkness of Elijah's depression.

Serving doesn't minimize our struggles, but it makes us realize that our struggles are not everything. Serving allows you to realize that moving forward is the best way to walk.

Finally, I often ask folks when they come in for couple's counseling how their marriage will better the world. I am sure Elisha and his calling faced the same type of one-on-one questioning with God.

The country and the church don't need to go backward. Instead, let's allow all women to wrestle with God in their own space, not by the rule of state or federal government.

Chapter 10
Let's Talk About Real Liberation
and Liberation Theology

"If you're telling a non-Black person about something racist that happened to you, make sure you are not bitter. Don't complain. Be forgiving. If possible, make it funny. Most of all, do not be angry. Black people are not supposed to be angry about racism. Otherwise you get no sympathy. This applies only for White liberals, by the way. Don't even bother telling a White conservative about anything racist that happened to you. Because the conservative will tell you that YOU are the real racist and your mouth will hang open in confusion."
—*Chimamanda Ngozi Adichie,* Americanah [1]

"I imagine one of the reasons people cling to their hates so stubbornly is because they sense, once hate is gone, they will be forced to deal with pain."
—*James Baldwin,* The Fire Next Time [2]

Sermon Site Media Tag: #MyBlackHistory The Real Battle Is Yet
To Come—The Hidden Cost of Liberation.
Contributed by Amiri Hooker, February 11, 2022
351 views
Scripture: Jeremiah 17:5-10
Denomination: United Methodist

About the sermon:
This final sermon of the book bridges the connection between justice and pov-

---

1. Chimamanda Ngozi Adichie, *Americanah* (Glasgow: HarperCollins UK, 2013).
2. James Baldwin, *The Fire Next Time* (New York: Modern Library, 1995).

erty and points to the question of why some folks are poor and others have so many resources. One of the main goals of this sermon is to look at the idea that Jeremiah was a prophet of equity over equality. Hopefully, the introduction to the powerful work of Heather McGhee gave the listener a view of justice that holds accountable those who are at the root cause of many of the major divides in our modern society. McGhee is an exceptional role model whose dedication to discussing liberation and racism has reshaped the conversation around these crucial issues. In her book *The Sum of Us: What Racism Costs Everyone and How We Can Prosper Together*, McGhee offers a solution-oriented vision for a more equitable society. She emphasizes that dismantling racism benefits everyone, as it fosters a society where everyone can thrive. Her ideas for practical, actionable change have inspired disciples and policy-makers alike.

While this sermon was not rejected by the sermon website, it appears it should have been rejected based on the moderators' previous comments. I believe it is worthwhile to include in this collection because it furthers the social justice and liberation theology concepts discussed throughout.

Excerpt of Approval:

"Amiri Hooker, your sermon #MyBlackHistory The Real Battle is Yet to Come— The Hidden Cost of Liberation, has been approved."

Reflection:

Sometimes approval is worse than rejection. A sermon on liberation and the battles for liberation and equality should raise flags on the evangelical Christian Nationalist radar. The lack of rejection might show that the sermon could have dealt more with the concepts of liberation.

Black preaching is not just an exercise in eloquence; it embodies a profound cultural heritage of racial uplift. By tapping into the rhythms, nuances, and symbols that define the African-American experience, Black preachers honor the struggles and triumphs of their ancestors while inspiring a collective sense of identity and pride. A sermon that is approved by an anti-liberative party might need to be more inspiring and more confrontational.

Striking a balance between promoting social justice and maintaining unity within religious communities is a formidable challenge. It requires a nuanced approach that respects diverse perspectives while upholding the principles of justice and equality. Encouraging open discussions and respecting the varying beliefs within religious circles can be a step toward finding common ground. Black liberation theology, a significant theological perspective that emerged in the 1960s, has played a pivotal role in shaping the mission and identity of the Black church. This real theology was forged in the crucible of the civil rights movement, a pivotal period marked by the quest for racial equality and the dismantling of institutionalized racism in the United States. At the forefront of this movement were leaders such as Dr. Martin Luther King Jr., Malcolm X, and a cadre of passionate activists who advocated for justice and equality. Emerging from these tumultuous times, theologians such as James Cone, J. Deotis Roberts, and Delores Williams began developing a theological framework that would reflect the Black church's unique struggle and experiences. They sought to reinterpret Christianity through the lens of the African-American experience, recognizing God as a liberator who sides with the oppressed and calls for social transformation.

Black liberation theology stands as a significant theological movement within the Black church, encouraging its members to find strength, hope, and a sense of purpose in their struggle against racial injustice. By prioritizing the liberation of the oppressed, fostering social activism, and celebrating the unique identity of African Americans, this theology has not only shaped the Black church but also made a profound impact on the broader fight for racial equality and justice. As we move forward, the principles of Black liberation theology continue to inspire communities to come together, advocating for a more inclusive and just society for all.

As the Black church continues to evolve and adapt to the changing times, the significance of Black power theology remains undeniable. By preaching this theology, the Black church continues to inspire its members to embrace their heritage, confront systemic injustices, and work collectively for a more equitable society. In doing so, the Black church upholds its historical legacy as a driving force for social change and empowerment within the African-American community.

Black history encompasses the experiences, accomplishments, and challenges faced by people of African descent throughout history. From the horrors of the transatlantic slave trade to the civil rights movement, Black history holds stories of resilience, determination, and triumph over adversity. This history is not just an isolated account; it is intertwined with the broader historical narrative of nations worldwide.

Education plays a pivotal role in shaping societal attitudes and beliefs. By including Black history in educational curricula, we promote awareness, understanding, and empathy for diverse cultures and backgrounds. Moreover, learning about historical figures such as King, Rosa Parks, Harriet Tubman, and countless others provides inspiration and empowers future generations to stand against injustice and discrimination. Embracing Black history encourages the celebration of diversity and inclusion within societies. It helps dismantle racial stereotypes and prejudices, leading to increased social harmony. By understanding the struggles and accomplishments of African Americans, people from different backgrounds can forge stronger connections, fostering a united and harmonious society. Black history provides an opportunity for societies to learn from past mistakes and progress toward a more equitable future.

Banning or ignoring this history hinders our ability to confront and learn from the injustices of the past. Acknowledging historical wrongs can help prevent their repetition and create a path toward a fairer and more just society for all.

The Sermon:
#MyBlackHistory The Real Battle is Yet to Come—The Hidden Cost of Liberation
By Amiri Hooker, February 11, 2022
Scripture: Jeremiah 17:5-10
Denomination: United Methodist

Scripture text:

Jeremiah 17:10 (NIV), "I the Lord search the heart and examine the mind, to reward each person according to their conduct, according to what their deeds deserve."

Introduction:

I am so blessed that I can tell the real Black history African-American story! Although it is great progress to have a Black History Month where everyone can learn about the contributions of Black Americans, it is also so very limiting.

Main body:

The narrative of Black people, as taught by most American schools, begins with slavery. But that's not where our story begins; our story begins in Africa. For each Black American, our story begins in a particular part of Africa, with an ethnic history, culture, and thriving community. I would like to suggest that this sets up a false divide that we see in the book of Jeremiah.

The book of Jeremiah is often associated with the prophet's concern for idolatry, the ways that Judah had forsaken Yahweh and turned to other gods.

The book of Jeremiah is primarily concerned with justice—to be exercised by rulers, to be sure, but also by all people. Importantly, then and now, survival in a time of crisis, according to the prophet, depends not on wisdom, might, and wealth but on fighting for justice for those on the social margins.

James Madison said it plainly in *The Federalist Papers* that justice is the protection of the weaker members of society from oppression by those more powerful.[3]

---

3. Alexander Hamilton, John Jay, and James Madison, *The Federalist Papers* (Redditch, UK: Read Books Ltd, 2018).

Point 1: While the book of Jeremiah places primary responsibility for executing justice upon kings, kings are not held exclusively responsible for justice.

The broader claim of the book of Jeremiah is that concern for justice is to permeate society and is a responsibility for all the people of Judah. God orders the prophet to search Jerusalem for even one person "who acts justly and seeks truth" (Jeremiah 5:1). The prophet's initial search is fruitless.

However, the initial search (5:1-3) was only among the poor, so God orders that the search continues among Jerusalem's leaders, "the rich" (v. 5). The results are no better, and the conclusion is that among both poor and rich alike "they do not know the way of the Lord, the requirements of their God" (v. 4-5 NIV).

The book of Jeremiah understands that God demands all persons in Judah—rich and poor, common citizens or monarch alike—to be attentive to God's demands for justice.

Because not a single person could be found in Jerusalem "who acts justly" (v. 1), the prophet warns that God will affect judgment instead of pardon (v. 6).

Point 2: An instrument of God's own judgment

In Chapter 17, the Babylonians are coming and will wreak havoc upon Judah and Jerusalem. Most readers of Jeremiah see the totality of the Babylonians' intentions and actions as the direct result of God's anger and vengeance toward Judah.

The text makes clear that God was most certainly involved in the coming of the Babylonians. This does not mean, however, that God created the Babylonian empire and armies and instilled therein a sense of vicious imperialism, all so it could be unleashed upon God's people at their first misstep. It has taken some time to understand that God has not made White supremacy or Christian nationalism.

Instead, God makes use of the already established regional policies and practices of the Babylonian empire as an instrument of God's own judgment and punishment against the deep and ongoing offenses of the people of Judah. Yes, the battle is not yours!

The people have invited the impending havoc upon themselves by their choices to turn away from the God of their ancestors, who created them, freed them from slavery, and gave them the land they inhabit.

Point 3: We are all in this history

You see, if we are going to celebrate Black history, we have to celebrate the good and the bad. Black History Month is not meant to pit Blacks and Whites against each other. And it's not meant to celebrate one race while excluding another. It's meant to highlight some of the important people and events of our American history.

Ignoring the past and pretending it didn't exist is not going to help us move forward with inclusion efforts.

I started this sermon by saying the rich and the poor were guilty of not doing justice. And I want to make it clear that the text points out that the fall of Judah and Jerusalem was about the oppressed and the oppressors not doing justice. Black History Month isn't simply about ethnic diversity in general but remembering the horrors of our shared history and celebrating the progress that has been made, in God's common kindness, and specifically the many successes of Black Americans despite such a history.

As David Mathis wrote, "Christians honor this month, at least in part, because it helps us understand the awful plight of a people made in God's image, many of them fellow believers, and acknowledges God's goodness at work in remarkable achievements … in and through a people who often have been treated with utter wickedness."[4]

Right now, there is a lot of anger in America. People are divided down political, religious, and even racial lines. Yet God has commanded us to put aside our prejudices and look at one another with his eyes. I have heard time and time again White folks say, "Well, where's our White history month?" I think this is the very issue Jeremiah was getting at when he condemns the rich and the poor.

Point 4: We rise or fall together

Let me see if I can modernize Jeremiah's point. We must abandon the notion that White people lose when Black people succeed. After decades of work in policy and economics, Heather McGhee says she eventually had a major realization: So many of this country's problems, from a decaying infrastructure to inadequate health care, stem from the false notion that success for people of color comes at the expense of White people.

Like Judah, "Our progress [as a nation] is being held back by a lie," McGhee said.[5]

In truth, we all rise or fall together, she said, citing research that the Black/White economic divide has cost the U.S. economy $16 trillion over the last 20 years.

McGhee added that during desegregation, communities often opted to close public pools rather than open them to Black people.

I don't think you heard that—they closed public swimming pools in the South,

4. David Mathis, "We Need Black History Month," *Desiring God*, February 1, 2017, https://www.desiringgod. org/articles/we-need-black-history-month.

5. Stacy Weiner, "Racism Hurts Us All, Warns Equity Activist Heather McGhee, JD," *AAMC*, June 29, 2022, https://www.aamc.org/news/racism-hurts-us-all-warns-equity-activist-heather-mcghee-jd.

places such as Kingstree, South Carolina, because the law changed that said they had to allow everyone to swim.

McGhee highlighted parallels in other aspects of American life, including a failure to support paid family leave, affordable housing, and access to a free or low-cost college education. Too often, efforts to advance such public goods stalled when many White people came to believe they primarily helped non-White people.

My grandmother used to say it another way: You don't cut off your nose to spite your face.

McGhee began to understand the economic issues that had always interested her as a kid—like why there were people asking for money on the street—were at their heart about race. In a White classmate's boast of being "socially liberal but fiscally conservative," she detected inherent stereotypes about whether Black people were deserving of the things White Americans had received for years.

Failing to acknowledge God as the source of good harvests, the people of Judah soon lost any sense of accountability to the Lord for how they worked. This led them to oppress and deceive the weak and defenseless. What ought to have been done for the good of all in God's land was done solely for individuals' own profit and without fear of their God for whom they were called to work. So, God withheld rain, and they soon learned that they were not the source of their own success.

God calls people to a higher purpose than economic self-interest. Our highest-end is our relationship with God, within which provision and material well-being are important, but limited, matters.

Jeremiah looked around and found that greed — the unbridled pursuit of economic gain — had displaced the love of God, as the people's chief concern.

As Walter Brueggemann states, "All persons, but especially the religious leaders, are indicted for their unprincipled economics. ... The people's hearts were inclined toward getting rich rather than fearing God and loving others."[6]

Point 5: Since its inception, Black History Month has never been just a celebration of Black America's achievements and stories.

It's part of a deliberate political strategy to be recognized as equal citizens. It's meant to show equality by providing equity.

Yet lost amid today's facile depictions of Harriet Tubman's Underground Railroad or George Washington Carver's peanuts is Black America's claim as coauthors of U.S. history, a petition the nation has never accepted.

This was the aim of Carter G. Woodson, historian and originator of Negro History Week in 1926. Like Jeremiah believed that appreciating a people's history was

6. Walter Brueggemann, *A Commentary on Jeremiah: Exile and Homecoming* (Grand Rapids, MI: W.B. Eerdmans, 1998).

a prerequisite to equality, Woodson wrote of the commemoration, "If a race has no history, if it has no worthwhile tradition, it becomes a negligible factor in the thought of the world."

That is, no amount of legislation can grant you equality if a nation doesn't value you.

Yes, church, I tell you the battle is still one we need valued action and policy.

But we must remember that Black History Month exists to deliver what federal policy has not—the eradication of systemic racism.

Yes, the policy is important, but the state of Black America today proves it is wholly insufficient on this score.

We have *Brown v. Board of Education*, yet the racial segregation of public schools remains the norm.

We have the Fair Housing Act, yet racial segregation in housing has barely changed in nearly four decades.

We have the Fifteenth Amendment and a Supreme Court-weakened Voting Rights Act, yet state laws still implement measures that disproportionately affect Black voters.

Black unemployment remains at twice the rate of White Americans.

Black median wealth is nearly ten times less than White wealth.

Black Americans are incarcerated at a rate five times that of their White countrymen.

And Black health continues to be worse on nearly every front—heart disease, asthma, infant mortality, diabetes—and the racial gap in cancer deaths is widening.

The time is now, America—to fight for both the rich and the poor to see and trust God.

Conclusion

We are at one of those moments when the American church needs to make a decision—or a decision will be made for us. The choices are clear: to ban Black history or to celebrate Black history. We stand at a crossroads, facing a decision that will shape our future.

The Black church and Black history sermons have played a pivotal role in America's spiritual awakening, challenging racial brutality and oppression, urging reflection about the sinful condition of racial segregation, and inviting Christians to grapple with brokenness within the body of Christ.

The sermons presented in this book—focusing on a historic cultural Jesus and collective theology—offer profound insights to readers, preachers, and lay servants. The banning and censorship of these sermons pose a threat to America's progress in time, faith, and democracy. Opponents, particularly Christian nationalists, fear that discussions about Black history and Critical Race Theory may evoke compassion for marginalized communities.

However, Black history is not confined to African Americans; it encompasses various Black communities throughout in the United States. To downplay Black history is to overlook the contributions of individuals, regardless of their race, who advocated for human rights and an end to discrimination. Those resistant to Black history sermons may fear a transformation of hearts, with some possibly apprehensive about the prospect of repentance.

Now is the time for us to stand up, aligning ourselves with love, justice, and righteousness, as our faith was born for such pivotal moments. A united opposition by people of faith against the exploitation of Christianity for nationalist, violent, and greedy purposes could wield significant influence.

What we need are sermons and teachings that usher in a political Pentecost and a comprehensive moral revival for the church, transcending political affiliations. The message of a Black Jesus and others in this book offer a resounding "no" to slavery, colonialism, apartheid, and racism, guiding our pursuit of justice.

The church must lead in addressing guilt and shame, confessing sins, seeking forgiveness, and fostering reconciliation. By acknowledging and celebrating Black history, we honor the resilience and contributions of Black brothers and sisters, fostering unity in the church.

A unified opposition by people of faith against the manipulation of Christianity could transform the world.

Appendix
Roll Call of Preachers Who
Might Be Banned #TA-DA

"Something has happened to Black people in these United States.
We are not as we were a few years ago, a few months ago, a few weeks ago.
Something has happened to us: not to America, but to us, to the way we think,
the way we fight, the way we work together. This is the most important thing that
has ever happened to America. What is that something? It is that fear is gone."
—The Reverend Albert Cleage Jr. [1]

Black sermons have always been more than just words spoken from the pulpit;
they are a source of empowerment for the congregation. In times of uncertainty and
upheaval, they provide a safe space for healing and hope. They offer guidance and
encouragement, urging us to draw on our faith to overcome obstacles and uplift our
communities. In the Black church tradition, sermons have long been a catalyst for
social justice and activism. Our preachers have stood at the forefront of the fight for
civil rights, using their sermons to inspire change and challenge the status quo.

In 2023, this tradition is more relevant than ever. In the face of systemic racism,
economic disparities, and social injustices, Black sermons have served as a rallying
cry for collective action, emphasizing the imperative to dismantle oppressive structures and cultivate a more just society.

There needs to be a roll call of Black history justice preachers who Christian nationalist and evangelical alt-right leaders and scribes would want banned.

The following is a personal collection of some of the Black history justice preachers who have sermons that have not been banned, thanks be to God. These are the

---

1. Albert B. Cleage, *The Black Messiah* (Chicago: Lushena Books, 1989).

preachers I read and listen to in looking to developing the sermons included in this collection.

The contemporary Black history preachers listed here have reinvigorated the art of preaching, breathing new life into traditional theology. By addressing the pressing issues of today through a spiritual lens, they have inspired countless individuals to engage actively in their communities and advocate for positive change. This is not a list of "who's who" of Black preachers or even a list of the best Black history justice preachers. This is a list of preachers I find a need to review and consult when I am in the study or going to a preaching event or protest rally.

Rev. Dr. Samuel DeWitt Proctor

In the realm of spiritual leadership, few figures stand as tall and influential as the Reverend Dr. Samuel DeWitt Proctor. A preacher's preacher, educator, civil rights activist, and personal mentor and friend, Proctor's impact on his generation was unparalleled.

Proctor's preaching was characterized by authenticity and conviction. He spoke from the heart, never afraid to confront uncomfortable truths or challenge the status quo. His sincerity resonated deeply with congregants, inspiring them to reflect on their own lives and seek meaningful change. As a master orator, Proctor captivated audiences with his eloquence and command of language. His sermons were not mere speeches; they were powerful narratives that wove together theology, history, and contemporary issues.

Proctor's exceptional qualities as a preacher made him a spiritual leader of his generation.

Rev. Dr. Gardner C. Taylor

Known as the "dean of Black preachers," the Reverend Dr. Gardner C. Taylor was a prominent pastor and civil rights advocate whose eloquence and oratory prowess captivated audiences around the world. His sermons transcended denominational boundaries and united people through their shared pursuit of justice and love. Taylor's powerful messages challenged the status quo and urged his listeners to confront racism, poverty, and inequality. His commitment to social justice and ecumenism played a pivotal role in fostering dialogue and understanding among diverse communities.

Bishop Vashti Murphy McKenzie

Breaking barriers as the first female bishop in the African Methodist Episcopal Church's history, Bishop Vashti Murphy McKenzie has been a trailblazer in advocating for gender equality within the church and society. Her leadership has provided a platform for women of faith to exercise their gifts and talents in ministry and leadership roles. McKenzie's sermons emphasize empowerment, self-worth, and social responsibility, inspiring her congregants to engage in acts of kindness and community service. Her dedication to bridging the gap between faith and social activism has impacted countless lives, creating a legacy of strong, empowered women who continue to change the world.

Rev. Dr. Jeremiah A. Wright Jr.

The Reverend Dr. Jeremiah A. Wright Jr. is renowned for his unapologetic critique of social injustices and systemic racism in America. As the former pastor of Trinity United Church of Christ in Chicago, he delivered sermons that addressed uncomfortable truths about the nation's history, calling for an honest reckoning with its past and a commitment to a more equitable future. Wright's sermons sparked intense debate and controversy but also ignited a necessary conversation about race and privilege. His commitment to challenging the status quo has inspired others to confront uncomfortable truths and work toward building a more just and inclusive society.

Rev. Zan Wesley Holmes Jr.

The Reverend Zan Wesley Holmes Jr.'s legacy is irrevocably linked to his relentless advocacy for civil rights. During the tumultuous times of the civil rights movement, he fearlessly stood at the forefront of the struggle for equality, championing the rights of African Americans and other marginalized communities. His courage in the face of adversity inspired countless individuals to stand up against injustice and discrimination. Among these luminaries stands the revered figure of Holmes. A visionary preacher, civil rights activist, and community leader, Holmes earned his place as one of America's greatest justice preachers. Throughout his illustrious career, Holmes consistently focused on empowering marginalized communities. As a justice preacher, he actively engaged with issues affecting the most vulnerable segments of society, such as poverty, access to education, and affordable housing.

Rev. Dr. Renita J. Weems

The Reverend Dr. Renita J. Weems is a powerful preacher and theologian who advocates for women's empowerment and gender equality. Her inspiring sermons challenge societal norms and encourage women to embrace their worth and potential in the eyes of God. Weems, a distinguished theologian, preacher, and writer, stands as an inspiring and influential figure in the realm of ministry. Her sermons and teachings have captivated audiences worldwide, leaving an indelible mark on the hearts and minds of countless individuals. At the core of Weems' preaching lies a strong emphasis on empowerment. Through her sermons, she has consistently sought to uplift and inspire individuals, especially women, to embrace their worth, potential, and agency. Weems empowers her listeners to see themselves as beloved children of God, worthy of respect and recognition in a world that may attempt to diminish their value. Weems is celebrated for her ability to address complex theological and ethical issues with grace and clarity. She fearlessly delves into topics that may be considered challenging or controversial, urging her congregants to wrestle with the complexities of faith and spirituality. An ardent advocate for social justice, Weems seamlessly weaves the pursuit of justice into her preaching. She challenges her listeners to confront systemic inequalities and embrace a collective responsibility to create a more just and compassionate society.

Rev. Hosea Williams

The Reverend Hosea Williams, a prominent United Methodist preacher and civil rights activist, played a significant role in the struggle for justice and equality during the civil rights movement. A close confidant of Dr. Martin Luther King Jr., Williams was known for his unwavering dedication to the principles of nonviolence and his tireless efforts in advancing civil rights for all. Williams's advocacy for justice aligned with the ideals of Dr. King. The two leaders collaborated closely in the civil rights movement, marching side by side and organizing protests for equal rights. Williams's ability to articulate the moral and spiritual imperative for justice made him an influential voice in the movement. His justice preaching was characterized by unyielding courage. He faced numerous threats, arrests, and physical attacks during his civil rights activism. Despite the dangers, Williams remained steadfast, using his pulpit to inspire others to stand up against injustice and systemic racism. Williams's justice preaching emphasized the power of nonviolent resistance as a means to bring about lasting change. He preached about the transformative impact of love, compassion, and forgiveness in the face of hatred and violence. Williams's sermons not only motivated individuals to take action but also inspired collective efforts to dismantle discriminatory practices.

Rev. Dr. Emilie M. Townes

The Reverend Dr. Emilie M. Townes is a towering figure in the realm of ministry, revered for her profound insights and unwavering commitment to social ethics. As a theologian, ethicist, and preacher, Townes's teachings have sparked thought-provoking discussions on justice, equality, and compassion. Her unique contribution to preaching lies in her seamless integration of theology and social ethics. Her sermons eloquently blend sacred texts with ethical considerations, shedding light on the moral imperatives that should guide our actions. By marrying spirituality with social responsibility, she inspires her audience to view justice and compassion as integral components of their faith journey. She recognizes that various forms of oppression intersect and compound, affecting marginalized communities differently. Her teachings emphasize the importance of addressing these interconnected issues and dismantling intersecting systems of power to create a more equitable society.

Rev. Dr. Pamela Lightsey

The Reverend Dr. Pamela Lightsey's preaching is rooted in a deep understanding of the gospel's central message of love, compassion, and justice. Drawing upon her own experiences as a Black queer woman, she challenges her listeners to confront systemic inequalities and discrimination head-on. Lightsey's sermons are not just spiritual reflections; they are a call to action for individuals and communities to actively engage in the pursuit of justice. As an openly queer woman, Lightsey has been a fearless advocate for LGBTQ+ rights within the church and beyond. Her justice preaching extends to fighting against homophobia and transphobia, pushing for greater acceptance and inclusion of LGBTQ+ individuals within religious communities. Her leadership has been instrumental in driving conversations about sexual orientation and gender identity within faith circles.

Rev. Dr. Otis Moss III

The Reverend Dr. Otis Moss III is a dynamic preacher whose sermons resonate with a diverse audience, transcending the boundaries of race, age, and denomination. As the senior pastor of Trinity United Church of Christ in Chicago, Moss infuses his sermons with a mix of social justice, cultural relevance, and biblical teachings. His thought-provoking messages address systemic inequalities, racism, and the need for spiritual transformation. Moss's approach to preaching reflects a commitment to empowering congregants to actively engage with the world beyond the sanctuary walls. By addressing contemporary issues through a theological lens, he encourages his listeners to be agents of change, pursuing justice and compassion in their daily lives. His influence has sparked a renewed interest in social gospel preaching, prompting other preachers to incorporate similar themes in their messages.

Rev. Dr. Neichelle Guidry

The Reverend Dr. Neichelle Guidry is a dynamic and visionary leader whose teaching and preaching draw upon womanist perspectives, incorporating the experiences of Black women into her biblical interpretations and addressing issues of race, gender, and class. Her unique blend of scholarship, spirituality, and social engagement has made her a prominent figure in contemporary religious circles. Guided by the principles of womanist theology, Guidry emphasizes the experiences and wisdom of Black women in her teachings. She believes that the transformative power of faith can bring healing to individuals and communities grappling with trauma and suffering. Her sermons are enriched by personal anecdotes, pop culture references, and historical context, making them accessible to people of diverse backgrounds and generations.

Rev. Dr. Marcus D. Cosby

The Reverend Dr. Marcus D. Cosby is celebrated for his passionate preaching style, charismatic delivery, and authentic engagement with his audience. As the senior pastor of Wheeler Avenue Baptist Church in Houston, Cosby emphasizes the transformative power of faith and its practical implications for living meaningful lives. With a focus on holistic development, Cosby's sermons address personal growth, emotional well-being, and community involvement. He weaves biblical principles into relatable stories, demonstrating how ancient wisdom is still relevant in navigating the complexities of contemporary life. His approach has inspired a generation of preachers to embrace a more relatable and application-focused style of preaching.

Rev. Dr. Bernice King

The Reverend Dr. Bernice King's justice preaching embodies the essence of her parents' legacy while paving a new path toward a more just and equitable society. The youngest child of civil rights leaders Martin Luther King Jr. and Coretta Scott King, her authenticity, intersectional approach, and commitment to nonviolence make her sermons resonate deeply with audiences across the globe. By fusing faith and social justice, she reminds us that spirituality and activism can work hand in hand to bring about transformative change. Her sermons advocate for nonviolent resistance as a transformative force that can break the cycle of hatred and violence. By embodying the principles of nonviolence, she inspires her listeners to respond to injustice with courage and grace.

Rev. Dr. Howard-John Wesley

As the pastor of Alfred Street Baptist Church in Alexandria, Virginia, the Reverend Dr. Howard-John Wesley is known for his authentic and transparent preaching. He tackles difficult subjects, such as mental health, economic disparities, and the role of faith in times of adversity, with unwavering honesty and compassion. Wesley's sermons offer a safe space for congregants to explore their doubts, fears, and hopes, fostering an environment of healing and support. His vulnerability has encouraged other preachers to be open about their own struggles, creating an atmosphere of empathy and authenticity within the pulpit.

Rev. Dr. Frederick Douglass Haynes III

We cannot overlook the powerful preaching of the street prophet. In the annals of African-American religious history, the legacy of the Reverend Dr. Frederick Douglass Haynes III stands tall as an indomitable force for positive change. As a prominent Black preacher, Haynes has consistently demonstrated a profound commitment to social justice, spiritual transformation, and community empowerment. The key to the empowerment that comes from the preaching of Haynes is his fearlessness. He is a fearless advocate for social justice. Haynes has courageously used his pulpit to address the pressing issues of social justice, inequality, and systemic racism. With a relentless passion for advocating for the marginalized and oppressed, his sermons echo the voices of those who have been silenced by society. Haynes refuses to shy away from difficult conversations, and his unapologetic approach to addressing social issues has inspired his congregants and audiences far beyond his church. Through his preaching, Haynes encourages congregants to take an active role in dismantling unjust systems and fostering equality. This type of follow-up after and during the sermon make it clear that his goal in the preached word is creating bold social justice disciples for Jesus Christ and the current church. Haynes stands as a beacon of hope, justice, and empowerment in the realm of Black preaching. His unyielding dedication to social justice, his inclusive approach to preaching, and his commitment to spiritual transformation make him one of the most-needed Black preachers of our time.

Bishop Rev. William Barber II

Bishop the Reverend William Barber II's significance as a preacher in the tradition of justice preaching cannot be overstated. His unwavering dedication to civil rights, advocacy for the marginalized, and the mobilization of the Moral Monday Movement showcase the true essence of justice preaching. By blending faith and activism, speaking truth to power, and serving as a bridge builder, Barber continues to inspire individuals to work toward a more equitable and just society. His legacy as an essential voice in the pursuit of social change serves as a beacon of hope for future generations, reminding us of all of the transformative power of justice preaching in shaping a better world.

Barber's preaching diverges from the traditional evangelical approach in several key ways. Unlike many traditional evangelicals who focus primarily on personal salvation and individual spirituality, Barber places significant emphasis on social justice and collective responsibility. His sermons address systemic issues such as poverty, racial discrimination, health care disparities, and voting rights. He believes that true faith should translate into tangible action to address societal ills and create a more equitable world.

Barber's theology is inclusive and embraces a broader understanding of Christianity. He emphasizes the principles of love, compassion, and justice as central tenets of the faith, inviting people of all backgrounds and beliefs to join the fight for a just society. He highlights the importance of addressing issues of race, class, gender, and other social identities as part of a comprehensive effort to achieve justice.

Barber's unique preaching has earned him the title "Jesus's poverty preacher" and a leadership place in the national conversation on civil rights and social change.

Bibliography

Adichie, Chimamanda Ngozi. *Americanah*. Glasgow: HarperCollins UK, 2013.

Ajayi, Luvvie. *I'm Judging You: The Do-Better Manual*. New York: Henry Holt, 2016.

Amsteus, Martin, Sarah Al-Shaaban, Emmy Wallin, and Sarah Sjöqvist. "Colors in Marketing: A Study of Color Associations and Context (in) Dependence." *International Journal of Business and Social Science 6, no. 3* (March 2015). https://ijbssnet.com/journals/Vol_6_No_3_March_2015/4.pdf.

Baldwin, James. *The Fire Next Time*. New York: Modern Library, 1995.

———. *The Price of the Ticket: Collected Nonfiction 1948-1985*. Boston: Beacon Press, 2021.

———. "The White Problem," in *The Cross of Redemption: Uncollected Writings*. Edited by Randall Kenan. New York: Vintage, 2011.

Bantu, Vince L. *A Multitude of All Peoples: Engaging Ancient Christianity's Global Identity*. Downers Grove, Ill.: IVP Academic, 2020.

Brueggemann, Walter. *A Commentary on Jeremiah: Exile and Homecoming*. Grand Rapids, Mich.: W.B. Eerdmans, 1998.

Brunwasser, Matthew. "Racism in Sudan." *The World*. PRI. February 7, 2011.

Cannon, Katie Geneva. *Teaching Preaching Isaac Rufus Clark and Black Sacred Rhetoric*. Eugene, OR: Cascade Books, 2015.

Cleage, Albert B. *The Black Messiah*. Chicago: Lushena Books, 1989.

Coates, Ta-Nehisi. *Between the World and Me*. London: One World, 2015.

Cohen, Sandy. "New Movie Shows Jesus as Black." *AP*. October 25, 2006. https://www.cbsnews.com/news/new-movie-shows-jesus-as-black.

Cone, James H. *Black Theology and Black Power*. Maryknoll, NY: Orbis Books, 1997.

———. *The Cross and the Lynching Tree.* Maryknoll, NY: Orbis Books, 2011.

Cordova, Randy. "Maya Angelou's 2011 'Arizona Republic' Interview." *The Arizona Republic.* May 28, 2014. https://www.azcentral.com/story/entertainment/books/2014/05/28/maya-angelou-arizona-republic-interview/9682587/.

Daniels III, David D. "1619 and the Arrival of African Christianity." *Jude 3 Project* (blog). August 31, 2019. https://jude3project.org/blog/slavetrade.

Diop, Cheikh Anta. *The African Origin of Civilization.* Edited by Mercer Cook. Chicago: Chicago Review Press, 1989.

"Doctoral Dissertations in Music and Music Education, 1968-1971." *Journal of Research in Music Education.* 20, no. 1 (1972): https://www.jstor.org/stable/i276042.

Earls, Aaron. "Pastors More Reluctant to Preach on Race." *Christianity Today.* January 12, 2021. https://www.christianitytoday.com/news/2021/january/pastors-reluctant-preach-racial-reconciliation-lifeway-surv.html.

Evans, Tony. "Race and Reconciliation (Sermon Only)." *YouTube.* December 2, 2020. https://www.youtube.com/watch?v=kW9LxQ33nZE.

Fisher, Earle J. *The Reverend Albert Cleage Jr. and the Black Prophetic Tradition: A Reintroduction of the Black Messiah.* New York: Lexington Books, 2021.

Garza, Alicia. *The Purpose of Power: How We Come Together When We Fall Apart.* London: One World, 2020.

Gay, Jerome. *The Whitewashing of Christianity: A Hidden Past, A Hurtful Present, and A Hopeful Future.* Chicago: 13th and Joan, 2021.

Grossu, Arina. "GROSSU: Margaret Sanger, Racist Eugenicist Extraordinaire." *The Washington Times.* May 5, 2014.

Hamilton, Alexander, John Jay, and James Madison, The Federalist Papers. Redditch, UK: Read Books Ltd, 2018.

Hammer, Joshua. *The Bad-Ass Librarians of Timbuktu: And Their Race to Save the*

World's Most Precious Manuscripts. New York: Simon and Schuster, 2016.

Hannah-Jones, Nikole, and The New York Times Magazine. *The 1619 Project: A New Origin Story*. Edited by Caitlin Roper, Ilena Silverman, and Jake Silverstein. New York: One World, 2021.

Hays, J. Daniel. "The Cushites: A Black Nation in Ancient History." *Bibliotheca Sacra* 153 (July 1996).

Hendricks Jr., Obery M. "'I Am the Holy Dope Dealer': The Problem with Gospel Music Today." *The Journal of the Interdenominational Theological Center* 27, Nos. 1 and 2 (Fall 1999/Spring 2000).

Humphries-Brooks, Stephenson. *Cinematic Savior: Hollywood's Making of the American Christ*. Westport, CT.: Praeger, 2006.

Kendi, Ibram X. *How to Be an Antiracist*. London: One World, 2019.

Lewis, Rep. John. Speaking on the George Floyd Justice in Policing Act. H.R. 7120. 116th Congress, *Congressional Record*, June 25, 2020.

Mandela, Nelson. *Long Walk to Freedom: The Autobiography of Nelson Mandela*. Boston: Little, Brown, 1994.

Mathis, David. "We Need Black History Month." *Desiring God*. February 1, 2017. https://www.desiringgod.org/articles/we-need-black-history-month.

Moore, Kristen R., David R. Williams, and Donna D. Baird. "Disparities by Skin Color among Young African-American Women." *Journal of Racial and Ethnic Health Disparities* 8, no. 4 (September 4, 2020). https://doi.org/10.1007/s40615-020-00856-x.

Morrison, Toni. "A Humanist View." Transcript of speech given at Portland State University Library. May 30, 1975. https://www.mackenzian.com/wp-content/uploads/2014/07/Transcript_PortlandState_TMorrison.pdf

Müller-Wille, Staffan. "Linnaeus and the Four Corners of the World." *The Cultural Politics of Blood, 1500–1900*. Editors Kimberly Anne Coles et al. London: Palgrave Macmillan, 2015.

Natanson, Hannah. "Her Students Reported Her for a Lesson on Race. Can She Trust Them Again?" *Washington Post*. September 18, 2023. https://www.washingtonpost.com/education/2023/09/18/south-carolina-teacher-ta-nehisi-coates-racism-lesson/.

Oden, Thomas C. *How Africa Shaped the Christian Mind: Rediscovering the African Seedbed of Western Christianity*. Westmont, Ill.: Intervarsity Press, 2010.

Perry, Tyler, dir. *Madea's Family Reunion*. Lionsgate. 2006.

Pratchett, Terry. *I Shall Wear Midnight*. New York: Random House, 2011.

Prince-Bythewood, Gina. "Director Gina Prince-Bythewood: Representation Still Too Rare in Hollywood (Guest Column)." *Variety*. February 27, 2020. https://variety.com/2020/artisans/opinion/black-history-month-director-gina-prince-bythewood-1203517648/.

Roberts, S. Craig, Roy C. Owen, and Jan Havlicek. "Distinguishing between Perceiver and Wearer Effects in Clothing Color-Associated Attributions." *Evolutionary Psychology*. July 1, 2020. https://doi.org/10.1177/147470491000800304.

Ruiz, Don Miguel, Don Jose Ruiz, and Janet Mills. *The Fifth Agreement*. San Rafael, CA.: Amber-Allen Publishing, 2010.

Schroeder, George. "Seminary Presidents Reaffirm BFM, Declare CRT Incompatible." *Baptist Press*. November 30, 2020. https://www.baptistpress.com/resource-library/news/seminary-presidents-reaffirm-bfm-declare-crt-incompatible/.

Shipp, E. R. "1619: 400 Years Ago, a Ship Arrived in Virginia, Bearing Human Cargo." *USA TODAY*. February 8, 2019.

Taylor, Juel, dir. *They Cloned Tyrone*. Netflix. 2023.

Thurman, Howard. *Jesus and the Disinherited*. Boston: Beacon Press, 2012.

Weiner, Stacy. "Racism Hurts Us All, Warns Equity Activist Heather McGhee, JD." *AAMC*. June 29, 2022. https://www.aamc.org/news/racism-hurts-us-all-warns-equity-activist-heather-mcghee-jd.

Williams, Theron D. *The Bible is Black History.* Indianapolis, IN: The Bible is Black History Institute, 2020.

Woodson, Carter Godwin. *The Mis-Education of the Negro.* London: Penguin Classics, 2023.

About the Author

A native of Philadelphia, Pennsylvania, and Bennettsville, South Carolina, Rev. Amiri B. Hooker received and accepted his calling in junior high school. He has been active in ministry thirty years. His immediate family includes his loving wife, Sgt. Valerie Hooker, oldest son Gabriyan, oldest daughter Sba Onesty Asha, youngest son Omri Charles-Bernard, and baby girl Sia Bari Ashira.

Hooker attended Methodist University in Fayetteville, North Carolina, at the encouragement of the late Bishop Joseph B. Bethea. There he majored in biblical studies, helped organized the State Black Student Network, and worked with the Children's Defense Fund and Black Community Crusade to help resurrect the Freedom Schools concept and the idea of racial uplift in young African-American adults.

After graduating with high honors from Methodist University, Hooker went on to enroll in a Master of Divinity program at the famed Gammon Division of the Inter-denominational Theological Center in Atlanta, Georgia, where he majored in theology with a concentration in African thought under the direction of Dr. Asa Hilliard.

During seminary, Hooker was ordained as a United Methodist pastor, received several awards, and was selected as a member of the Association for the Study of Classical African Civilizations. Hooker has prophetically served churches he has been appointed to in various ways. He has faithfully served the South Carolina Annual Conference as a Bishop Joseph Bethea Award winner, Advocacy Convener and chair of the inaugural Racial Reconciliation Design Team. He has also partnered with schools, Head Start, and minister's groups. He serves as a board member of the South Carolina Christian Action Council and the National African American Ministers Leadership Council as the chair of the MICAH Group and is one of the tri-chairs in the South Carolina division of the Poor People's Campaign. He is also a member of the National Association for the Advancement of Colored People and Black Methodists for Church Renewal.

Yet the simple truth is best. If asked, he says, "I am just a child of God, called by God."

"For the appeal we make does not spring from error or impure motives,
nor are we trying to trick you. On the contrary, we speak as those
approved by God to be entrusted with the gospel. We are not trying to please people
but God, who tests our hearts."—1 Thessalonians 2:3-4, NIV

www.ingramcontent.com/pod-product-compliance
Lightning Source LLC
Chambersburg PA
CBHW051430090426
42737CB00014B/2910